⊛ Science in a Social Context

Limits of a Modern World

A Study of the
'Limits to Growth' Debate

Robert McCutcheon
History and Social Studies of Science
University of Sussex

Butterworths
LONDON - BOSTON
Sydney - Wellington - Durban - Toronto

The Butterworth Group

United Kingdom London	Butterworth & Co (Publishers) Ltd 88 Kingsway, WC2B 6AB
Australia Sydney	Butterworths Pty Ltd 586 Pacific Highway, Chatswood, NSW 2067 Also at Melbourne, Brisbane, Adelaide and Perth
Canada Toronto	Butterworth & Co (Canada) Ltd 2265 Midland Avenue, Scarborough, Ontario, M1P 4S1
New Zealand Wellington	Butterworths of New Zealand Ltd T & W Young Building, 77—85 Customhouse Quay, 1, CPO Box 472
South Africa Durban	Butterworth & Co (South Africa) (Pty) Ltd 152—154 Gale Street
USA Boston	Butterworth (Publishers) Inc 19 Cummings Park, Woburn, Mass. 01801

© SISCON 1979
First published 1979
ISBN 0 408 71310 0

British Library Cataloguing in Publication Data

McCutcheon, Robert
    Limits of a modern world.
    1. Science — Social aspects. 2. Technology —
    Social aspects.
    I. Title II. Science in a Social Context
    (Project)
    301.24'3   Q175.5   78-41270

    ISBN 0-408-71310-0

Typeset by Butterworth Litho Preparation Department
Printed in England by Billing and Sons Ltd,
Guildford and London

Chapter One
Limits to Growth

1. Introduction

> The explosive growth of the human population is the most
> significant terrestrial event of the past million millenia . . . No
> geological event in a billion years — not the emergence of mighty
> mountain ranges, nor the submergence of entire subcontinents,
> nor the occurrence of periodic glacial ages — has posed a threat to
> terrestrial life comparable to that of human overpopulation.
>
> Paul Ehrlich

> The principal defect of the industrial way of life, with its ethos
> of expansion is that it is not sustainable. Its termination within
> the lifetime of someone born today is inevitable — unless it
> continues to be sustained for a while longer by an entrenched
> minority at the cost of imposing great suffering on the rest of
> mankind. We can be certain, however, that sooner or later it will
> end (only the precise time and circumstances are in doubt) and
> that it will do so in one of two ways: either against our will, in a
> succession of famines, epidemics, social crises and wars; or because
> we want it to — because we wish to create a society which will
> not impose hardship and cruelty upon our children — in a
> succession of thoughtful humane and measured changes.
>
> *A Blueprint for Survival*

> We have been massively intervening in the environment without
> being aware of many of the harmful consequences of our acts
> until they have been performed and the effects — which are
> difficult to understand and sometimes irreversible — are upon us.
> Like the Sorcerer's apprentice, we are acting upon dangerously
> incomplete knowledge. We are, in effect, conducting a huge
> experiment *on ourselves.* A generation hence — too late to help —
> public health statistics may reveal what hazards are associated
> with these pollutants.
>
> Barry Commoner

These quotations display the crisis that is seen to exist in at least four
areas of importance to man: population; food and other resources; the
methods of producing food, resources and commodities; and the
pollution caused by the interaction of these factors. There have been
many books, critics, TV films and talk shows on these and related
topics in recent years. A mass of evidence and theory has been presented
on almost every aspect of the subject.

One of the most widely read and discussed books on the subject has been *The Limits to Growth*, which was written at the Massachusetts Institute of Technology (MIT) by a team of experts, under the direction of Dennis Meadows. Popular editions of the book have sold nearly 2 million copies throughout the world. Many works written since its publication in 1972 have quoted the conclusions of *The Limits to Growth* as one of the starting points in their own analyses. For example, R. Heilbroner, *The Human Prospect*; John Passmore, *Man's Responsibility for Nature*; and *The Blueprint for Survival*.

In their book *Global Simulation Models*, Cole and Clark have given five reasons for the wide ranging impact of *The Limits to Growth*:

(a) It came at a time of increasing concern with issues of pollution, famine and overpopulation, and, to a lesser extent resource shortages on a local and global scale.

(b) The work was carried out at the Massachusetts Institute, one of the foremost technological institutes in the world.

(c) The use of a computer and computerized output gave additional respectability to the work and enhanced the apparent objectivity of the analysis.

(d) The Club of Rome, as an influential and active organization, was an important factor in initial acceptance.

(e) Perhaps the most significant factor, apart from timeliness, was the marketing of *The Limits to Growth* by the publishers Potomac Associates. According to the journal *Science* (March 10, 1972), 12,000 copies of *The Limits to Growth* were sent to influential government and political leaders and personal visits were made to them by The Club of Rome members and by Meadows and his colleagues. The work received wide media attention. The model was originally presented at the Smithsonian Institute to a distinguished invited audience of academics, ambassadors and other high level government officials, and later at US Embassies in the UK and elsewhere. As mentioned above nearly two million copies have been sold throughout the world.

For these reasons — its timeliness, its pedigree, its influence and its publication sales — we have chosen to use *The Limits to Growth* as a means of introducing discussion of population growth, food, non-renewable resources and pollution. We will begin by describing some of the factors which led to the publication of *The Limits to Growth*. Following this introduction we will outline the main arguments presented in the book.

In Chapter One we are summarizing *The Limits to Growth* with only minimal comment. In following chapters we look at its content and methodology in greater detail and more critically. So the description in this chapter of some aspects of *The Limits to Growth* without comment or criticism should not be taken to imply approval or agreement, it is merely a *statement* of what is in the book.

2. Events leading to the publication of 'The Limits to Growth'

During the 1960s concern about the effects of industrial activity upon the environment developed into an 'environmental movement'. This movement gained particular strength in the USA and can perhaps be dated from 1962 with the publication of Rachel Carson's *Silent Spring*, which was the first popular account of the dangerous effects of pesticides on wild life. With the growth of this concern, the writings of those who were most acquainted with the effects upon the environment were more widely read. The writings of Paul Ehrlich, *The Population Bomb*, and Barry Commoner, *The Closing Circle*, became best sellers. The important point to note is that the vast majority of this literature was pessimistic about the future of man.

Whether as a response to this development or not, another development was taking place — people began to be sceptical that continued economic growth would eventually increase everyone's 'quality of life'. To the contrary, it began to be said that growth often impaired the quality of life. The concern over the deteriorating environment began to be linked to unbridled economic growth and both were seen to be involved with the problems of population increase, urbanization, international conflict and the depletion of natural resources.

During the 1960s, Aurelio Peccei, who has been the vice-chairman of both Fiat and Olivetti and the chief executive of Olivetti, became increasingly concerned with the effects of these phenomena. In 1969 he published a book *The Chasm Ahead* in which he wrote:

> Phenomenal increases, rapidly approaching critical maxima along exponential curves, are happening in population, pollution, energy release . . . In the changed/dynamics of these interacting factors lie the reasons why mankind is confronted with such an unprecedented complex of problems . . . new generations openly contest the views and deeds of older ones, leadership is wanting, no inspiring leadership is surging to the forefront . . .

He felt that problems which were international and global in scope could not be solved through national efforts. The reason, he wrote early in his book, was that

> . . . the outdated and inefficient socio-political organisation is patently incapable of coping with the new pattern of forces which have emerged in the modern age.

In 1966 Peccei had concluded that a study of world problems should be initiated. He travelled widely in Europe, America and the Soviet Union trying to interest people in sponsoring his project. He met with little more than polite interest. However, in 1968 after consulting

Alexander King (the Scientific Director of the Organization for Economic Cooperation and Development) and Eric Jantsch (who has written on technological forecasting for the OECD), Peccei obtained the sponsorship of the Giovanni Agnelli Foundation (Agnelli is the chairman of Fiat). In April 1968, a meeting was held in Rome, and to it were invited 'economists, planners, geneticists, sociologists, politologues and managers'. Apparently this meeting was not too successful as the invited guests were not able to think of global analysis. Undaunted, Peccei persevered and with the support of five others founded the Club of Rome in April 1968. The secretariat of the Club is located in Rome and it has offices in Geneva and Tokyo. However, although the Club had decided that it wished to look at the problems from a global perspective, it did not know which method to follow in tackling such a huge task.

One of the members of the Club, Professor Carroll Wilson of MIT, suggested that a colleague of his at MIT — Jay Forrester, the Professor of Management at the Alfred P. Sloan School of Management — had developed a method of examining complex systems. The method was 'systems dynamics'.

Systems dynamics had grown out of the systems approach. Briefly, 'a systems approach to problems demands that a piecemeal approach is replaced by an overall approach'. It has a long history and its roots can be traced to the writings of ancient philosophers who held that 'the whole is greater than the sum of its parts'. The recent growth in importance of the systems approach stems from several sources. In the Second World War various sophisticated mathematical techniques were developed for the operation of new weapons and weapons systems (operations research). Similar methods have been used throughout the post-war period in relation to space programs and the management of large business companies.

Perhaps the biggest impetus to the rise in importance of the systems approach has been the rapid development of the electronic computer. Complex mathematical relationships could now be resolved at great speed. It became feasible to study the dynamic behavior of complex interacting systems, provided that appropriate parameters could be identified, quantified and related to one another.

This combination of a systems approach to complex systems, mathematical methods of relating the parameters of a system developed in operations research, and the ability of the modern computer to calculate the results of complex equations, was developed into 'systems dynamics' at MIT. One of the first applications of systems dynamics was to a description of the functioning of industrial concerns by the Sloan School of Management at MIT, under the direction of Jay W. Forrester, whose book, *Industrial Dynamics*, was published in 1962.

The method began to be widely used in industrial and other fields. In 1969 Forrester applied it to urban studies: *Urban Dynamics*. And it began to be felt by many that the complex nature of Government planning policy might be unravelled using the systems approach. For example, in the late sixties the Vice-President of the USA, Hubert Humphrey, said that in order to 'clean up the cities . . . the systems analysis approach that we have used in our space and aeronautic program' would be necessary.

In 1970, Forrester, on the recommendation of Carroll Wilson, was invited to give a presentation of his work to the Club of Rome. He committed himself tentatively to the project after a Club meeting in Berne on 29 June 1970, 'that momentous day when it all began', Wilson said. Later that summer, at a two week long meeting, Forrester presented a systems dynamics world model (published in 1971 as *World Dynamics*). It was agreed to use this method for the Project on the Predicament of Mankind, and funds were obtained so that Forrester's associate, Dennis L. Meadows could develop a more sophisticated analysis, which was published early in 1972: *The Limits to Growth*.

The book itself is really only a description of the approach taken by the team under Dennis Meadows and a discussion of the conclusions reached. The actual equations and data used by the team can be found in their Technical Report which was published later (*ref. 1.14*).

At this point before continuing further, you are encouraged (a) to read *The Limits to Growth* thoroughly and (b) to examine the assumptions and methods used by the experts and the conclusions reached by them. Following such an examination it is hoped that you will discuss the advantages and limitations of *The Limits to Growth* and clearly set out to show whether you agree or disagree with the MIT study. The seminar questions at the end of this chapter might prove useful here. What follows is what I consider to be the main argument employed by Meadows and his team. I have made very few comments during the precis of their work, those comments which have been made are in brackets.

3. The Limits to Growth

(a) THE OBJECT OF THE INQUIRY

In their introduction the authors state that their world model was built 'specifically to investigate five major trends of global concern — accelerating industrialization, rapid population growth, widespread malnutrition, depletion of non-renewable resources, and a deteriorating environment'. The object of the investigation was to answer the following set of questions:

Are the implications of the global trends so threatening that their resolution should take precedence over local, short-term concerns?

Is it true, as U Thant (the late Secretary-General of the United Nations) suggested, that there remains less than a decade to bring these threats under control?

If they are not brought under control, what will the consequences be?

What methods does mankind have for solving global problems and what will be the results and costs of employing each of them?

(b) THE METHOD OF INQUIRY I

The method by which the team approached the problem of understanding the causes and predicting the consequences of these trends of global importance was a formal written model expressed in mathematical terms. In principle this formal model combined the body of known information with the new information processing tools that have been produced: the scientific method, systems analysis and the computer. They saw this as the means to overcome the limitations of traditional approaches which focussed upon isolated factors instead of the 'full catastrophe'.

In addition, the advantages of this formal model over mental models are said to be: (1) every assumption is written in a precise form so that it is open to inspection and criticism; (2) after the assumptions have been criticised and used their implications for the future behavior of the world system can be traced without error by a computer.

The authors begin by stating that population, food production, industrialization, pollution and consumption of non-renewable natural resources are all increasing at an exponential rate. The impressive thing about quantities increasing at an exponential rate is the speed at which they can double, if the rate at which they are growing is high.

Systems dynamics has shown the authors that any exponentially growing quantity is involved with a positive feedback loop i.e. the outcome of an event directly and positively influences the next occurrence of the event itself. Hence, in beginning their 'dynamic analysis' of the five factors named above, the authors set themselves the task of locating the positive feedback loops underlying the exponential growth rates which have been observed (and commenting upon the implications of each trend considered separately from the others).

(c) CAUSES AND IMPLICATIONS OF EXPONENTIAL GROWTH

(i) Population: Population is growing at 2.1% per year. The positive feedback loop is the number of births per year and depends upon the average (achieved) fertility and the length of delay between generations. The negative feedback loop — the number of deaths per year — opposes the positive feedback loop. The cause of the recent super exponential

rise in world population is that, whereas there has been a slight decrease in birth rates, there has been a marked decrease in death rates. The decrease in death rates has been caused by the spread of modern medicine, public health techniques and the new methods of growing and distributing food.

How does this affect the future? There is extreme difficulty in controlling the positive feedback loop (birth rates), since most of the prospective parents of the year 2000 have already been born, by which time the authors predict a population of about 7 billion.

(ii) Industrial Production: Industrial production is growing at 5% per year. Industrial output results from industrial capital (equipment) being invested in industry. The products of industry are consumer goods, which leave the industrial system, and capital goods (i.e. machines capable of making either consumer goods or other machines) which contribute to further output. This production of capital goods comprises the positive feedback loop. But capital goods wear out (depreciate) — the negative feedback loop. The present exponential growth of industry results from the fact that capital goods are being produced faster than they wear out (or at least faster than they are replaced).

After their examination of the positive feedback loops operating in population and industrial production the authors ask:

> Can the growth rates of population and capital . . . be physically sustained in the world? How many people can be provided for on this earth, at what level of wealth and for how long? To answer these questions we must look in detail at those systems in the world which provide the physical support for population and economic growth.

In beginning to look at these systems the authors state that two main categories of ingredients are necessary to sustain world economic growth: physical (food, raw materials, ecological systems) and social (peace and social stability, education and employment, and steady technological progress). They stress that neither the book nor the world model dealt with social factors. The physical factors are examined assuming that the best possible social conditions prevail, (later in the Commentary, the executive committee of the Club of Rome write:

> the limits to growth it examines are only the known uppermost physical limits imposed by the finiteness of the world system. In reality, these limits are further reduced by political, social and institutional constraints, by inequitable distribution of population and resources, and by our inability to manage very large intricate systems.

9

This reinforces the impression created that social factors can only worsen the situation. The MIT team are therefore only examining what they consider to be the most optimistic of possibilities: the absolute maximum lies in the physical limits).

(iii) Food: The exponential growth of demand for food results directly from the positive feedback loop that is now determining the growth of human population. One third of the world's population is inadequately nourished. World food production is increasing but food production per capita in the non-industrialized countries is barely holding constant. Do these rather dismal statistics mean that the limits of food production on earth have already been reached?

The primary resource for producing food is land. On the world's surface there are, at most, 3.2 billion hectares of land potentially suitable for agriculture. Approximately half of that land is under cultivation today. The costs of developing the remaining land (roads, clearing, irrigation, fertilizing) are high; average cost for opening land in unsettled areas has been $1150 per hectare. An FAO report states that it is not economically feasible to open more land to cultivation.

But assuming that each person needs 0.4 ha (present world average) and that all the available land can be utilized, the limit to food production sustaining the rising population is reached about the year 2000. Further, that even if we double or quadruple the present productivity of land each doubling only postpones collapse by about 30 years. The present 10 to 20 million deaths due to malnutrition are a forewarning of the land shortage that is already being felt in various parts of the world. Many of these deaths are due to social limitations rather than physical ones but if good fertile land were still easily reached and brought under cultivation, there would be no economic barrier to feeding the hungry.

(iv) Non-renewable resources: Since the usage rate is growing faster than population, it is driven by the positive feedback loops of both population and industrial growth. A list of some of the vital raw materials for major industrial processes is given — together with known global reserves, the static reserve life index and the growth rate over the last few years. Using chromium as an example (because it has one of the longest static reserve indices) the authors conclude: 'Given the present resource consumption rates and the projected increase in those rates, the great majority of the currently important non-renewable resources will be extremely costly 100 years from now'. They hold that the statement remains true regardless of the most optimistic assumptions about undiscovered reserves, technological advances, substitution or recycling — as long as the demand continues to grow exponentially.

(v) Pollution: Scientific attempts to measure the effort of industrial activity upon the natural environment have been limited. The authors

make four points which illustrate the difficulty in understanding and controlling the future state of our ecological systems:

(a) The few kinds of pollution that have been measured over time seem to be increasing exponentially. They are influenced by both the population and the industrial feedback loops.

(b) We have almost no knowledge of where the upper limits to the pollution curves might be.

(c) The presence of natural delays in ecological processes, increases the probability of underestimating the control measures necessary and therefore of inadvertently reaching the upper limits.

(d) Many pollutants are globally distributed; their harmful effects appear at long distances from their points of generation. A characteristic of many pollutants is their ability to become widely distributed about the land.

The authors' conclusions with respect to pollution are that it is difficult to estimate exactly how fast the exponential curve of total pollution release is rising. The precise limit to the earth's ability to absorb any single kind of pollution is unknown, let alone a combination of pollutants. However, this upper limit has been surpassed in many local environments and they therefore state, 'We do know however that there is an upper limit . . . the surest way to reach that upper limit globally is to increase exponentially both the number of people and the polluting activities of each person'.

The authors conclude their investigation of the causes of exponential growth and the implications of present trends with the following:

> The apparent goal of the present world system is to produce more people with more (food, material goods, clean air and water) for each person. In this chapter we have noted that if society continues to strive for that goal, it will eventually meet one of its many earthly limitations . . . the short doubling times of many of man's activities, combined with the immense quantities being doubled, will bring us close to the limits to growth of those activities surprisingly soon.

(d) THE METHOD OF INQUIRY II

Having first examined the data related to the five factors under consideration and then the causes of exponential growth and its implications in each of the five fields, taken separately, the authors now address themselves to the results obtained when all five factors are interacting simultaneously, as in a real world situation. In what way will the conclusions reached in relation to the individual factors be altered by considering the interactions of all five at once?

Systems dynamics has shown the authors that it is impossible to

11

understand, intuitively, the interaction of these five factors. To obtain an understanding a formal (mathematical) world model was built. Their major purpose of the world model is to ascertain the behavior modes of the population capital system as it reaches the limits to growth. By behavior mode is meant whether a variable increases, decreases, remains constant, oscillates, or combines several of these characteristic modes.

The steps used in constructing the model were:

1. The important causal relationships among the five levels were listed and the feedback loop structures traced ... 'the most basic structures' were sought;
2. These relationships were then quantified;
3. With a computer they calculated the simultaneous operation of all these relationships over time;
4. Finally they tested the effect on this global system of various policies that are currently being proposed to enhance or change the behavior of the system.

Because they are only interested in the world system's behavioral tendencies they aggregated their data: one general population – a population that statistically reflects the average characteristics of the global population; one class of pollutants – the long-lived globally distributed family of pollutants, such as lead, mercury, asbestos and the stable pesticides and radioisotopes – whose dynamic behavior in the environment is beginning to be understood; one generalized resource that represents the combined reserves of all non-renewable resources. The authors acknowledge that a model based on such a high level of aggregation cannot make exact predictions but they assert:

> On the one hand it is vitally important to gain some under- standing of the causes of growth in human society, the limits to growth, and the behaviour of our socio-economic systems when the limits are reached. Man's knowledge of the behaviour modes of these systems is very incomplete. It is currently not known, for example, whether the human population will continue growing, or gradually level off, or oscillate around some upper limit or collapse. We believe that the aggregated world model is one way to approach such questions.

They then outline the basic structure of the model in a graphic form and the various feedback loops that comprise the links between the various components but they do not give the mathematical relation- ships which are used in the actual computer runs themselves (these are published in the Technical Report).

As to the accuracy of the data used in these mathematical relationships they state, 'The current state of knowledge about causal relationships in the world ranges from complete ignorance to extreme accuracy. The relationships in the world model generally fall in the middle ground of certainty'. Having admitted the difficulty in obtaining data for many of the relationships they still feel confident that 'even in the absence of improved data, information now available is sufficient to generate valid basic behavior modes for the world system. This is true because the model's feedback loop structure is a much more important determinant of overall behavior than the exact numbers used to quantify the feedback loops.' Even as such, 'our only alternatives to a model like this, based on partial knowledge, are mental models, based on the mixture of incomplete information and intuition that currently lies behind most political decisions'. (Allowing this point, the sensitivity of the model to the choice of the numerical values used in the feedback loops is an important consideration to which we shall return in Chapter 6, section 2.)

(e) WORLD MODEL BEHAVIOR

After ascertaining data for the original factors, determining the feedback loops governing them, the interactions between the five factors, and ascertaining data for these interactions, the model is finally constructed and run. (See figures 24 and 25 on pp. 97 and 100.)

The 'standard run' assumes that there will be no great changes in human values or the functioning of the global population industrial system as it has operated for the last one hundred years, (see figure 35 on p. 124). The authors find that the basic mode of behavior is 'overshoot and collapse' through depletion of non-renewable resources: 'We can thus say with some confidence that, under the assumption of no major change in the present system, population and industrial growth will certainly stop within the next century at the latest'.

Doubling the supply of resources leads to a similar form of 'overshoot and collapse'. But this time it is due to pollution (figure 36, p. 127).

The authors next examine the contention that the application of new technology to the various problems of overpopulation, food production, discovery of new resources and energy would allow the growth of population and industrial development to continue. For example, resource availability is quadrupled. But no amount of fiddling with the quantities of food, resources and pollution has any substantial effect; it only delays matters slightly.

The basic behavior mode of the world system is exponential growth of population, followed by collapse.

(f) THE STABLE STATE

In the final chapter the authors discuss the alterations to the model relationships which would have to be made to stave off imminent disaster. Their objective is a stable state which is (1) sustainable without sudden and incontrollable collapse and (2) capable of satisfying the basic material requirements of all its people.

By weakening the positive feedback loops of both population and industrial growth and by introducing technological changes they discover that it is possible to achieve a stable state (relatively). A minimum set of requirements for the state of stable equilibrium are then given. However, they consider that this weakening of the positive feedback loops can only take place through the means of policy i.e. by non-technical means.

Their conclusions to the investigation into the 'five major trends of global concern' were,

> If the present trends in world population, industrialisation, pollution, food production, and resource depletion continue unchanged, the limits to growth on this planet will be reached sometime within the next one hundred years. The most probable result will be a rather sudden and uncontrollable decline in both population and industrial capacity.

The object of this investigation was to answer a set of questions related to the possibilities of averting such a crisis. From their analysis their answers to that set of questions (p. 20) are contained in the following statements:

> It is possible to alter these growth trends and to establish a condition of economic stability that is sustainable far into the future. The state of global equilibrium could be designed so that the basic material needs of each person on earth are satisfied and each person has an equal opportunity to realise his individual human potential. If the world's people decide to strive for this second outcome rather than the first, the sooner they begin working to attain it, the greater will be their chance of success.

And they conclude

> With that goal and that commitment (to the achieving of the stable state), mankind would be ready now to begin a controlled, orderly transition from growth to global equilibrium.

Reading

ESSENTIAL

1.1   Meadows, Dennis H. *et al.* (1972). *The Limits to Growth*, Potomac Associates, and London, Pan Books, 1974.

(Readers are urged to refrain from reading the following material until they have read *The Limits to Growth* and formed their own opinions about the various issues raised.)

1.2   Clark, John and Cole, Sam, *Global Simulation Models.* John Wiley, 1975.

1.3   Cole, H. S. D., Freeman, Christopher, Jahoda, Marie and Pavitt, K. L. R., *Thinking about the Future: A Critique of The Limits to Growth.* Chatto and Windus, 1973.

1.4   Commoner, Barry, *The Closing Circle.* Jonathan Cape, 1972; Chapters 1 and 2.

1.5   The Ecologist, *A Blueprint for Survival.* Penguin, 1972, pp. 15–29.

1.6   Ehrlich, Paul, *The Population Bomb.* Ballantine, 1971.

1.7   Forrester, Jay W., *World Dynamics.* Wright Allen, 1971.

1.8   Freeman, C. and Jahoda, M. (eds.), *World Futures: the great debate.* London, Martin Robertson, 1978.

1.9   Gillette, Robert, 'The Limits to Growth: Hardsell for a Computer view of Doomsday', *Science,* 175, 10th March 1972, pp. 1088–1092.

1.10 Heilbroner, Robert, *An Inquiry into the Human Prospect.* W. W. Norton, 1974, pp. 13–58.

1.11 Herrera, A. *et al., Catastrophe or New Society?* Ottawa: IDRC for the Fundacion Bariloche, 1976.

1.12 Kahn, Herman, Brown, William and Martel, Leon, *The Next 200 Years.* London Associated Business Programmes, 1977.
      '. . . 200 years ago almost everywhere human beings were comparatively few, poor and at the mercy of the forces of nature, and 200 years from now, we expect, almost every-where they will be numerous, rich and in control of the forces of nature . . .'

1.13 Leontief, W. *et al., The Future of the World Economy —Preliminary Report.* UN NY, 1976.

1.14 Meadows, Dennis L. *et al., Dynamics of Growth in a Finite World.* Wright Allen, 1974. 637 page Technical Report.

1.15 Meadows, Dennis L. *et al., Towards Global Equilibrium: Collected Papers.* Wright Allen, 1973.

1.16 Mesarovic, Mihajlo and Pestel, Eduard, *Mankind at the Turning Point: The Second Report of the Club of Rome.* E. P. Dutton & Co/Readers Digest Press, 1974.
      'Our scientifically conducted analysis of the long-term world development based on all available data points out quite clearly that such a passive course leads to disaster . . . All contem-porary experience thus points to the reality of an emerging world system.'

1.17 Simmons, Harvey, 'Systems Dynamics and Technocracy', in Cole *et al.*, 1973 (see *1.3* above) pp. 192–208.

1.18 Tinbergen, Jan (coordinator), Dolman, A. J. (editor), *Reshaping the International Order. A report to the Club of Rome.* E. P. Dutton & Co, 1976.

'. . . what new international order should be recommended to the world's statesmen and social groups so as to meet, to the extent practically and realistically possible, the urgent needs of today's population and the probable needs of future generations.'

JOURNALS WHICH OFTEN CONTAIN ARTICLES RELEVANT TO THESE TOPICS

Bulletin of the Atomic Scientists, Economist, Environment, Futures, Futurist, Impact of Science in Society, Nature, New Internationalist, New York Review of Books, New Scientist, Science, Scientific American, Science for the People, STPP News (PURDUE), Technological Forecasting and Social Change, Technology and Culture.

In addition to these journals most newspapers have printed frequent articles on one or other aspect of the debate. It would be worthwhile collecting several of these articles and subjecting them to analysis in relation to:

(a) the scope of the article
(b) the evidence upon which it is based
(c) the method which it uses to reach its conclusions
(d) the conclusions
(e) the policy recommendations
(f) the means by which the policies will be effected.

A 'Horizon' television program is particularly appropriate to this chapter:

'Due to lack of interest tomorrow has been cancelled', Producer Michael Barnes *BBC Enterprises Hire Catalogue*, 1973–4.

Points for discussion or essays

1. Describe in detail the model used to investigate *The Limits to Growth*.
2. What are the causes of exponential growth discussed in *The Limits to Growth*?
3. Are the factors examined by the authors the ones which 'determine and therefore, ultimately limit growth'?
4. In relation to the following questions discuss firstly the opinions in *The Limits to Growth* and then your own appraisal:

(a) What are the 'five trends of global concern'? Are these the driving force in the world today? If so, why?

(b) Are there any trends which might oppose the direction of the 'five'?

(c) Are the trends continuing?

(d) If so, are they subject to alteration?

(e) If not, are we absolutely doomed?

5. Discuss the methods which have been used to construct the model. What role is played by scientific method?

6. What are the conclusions reached by the authors of *The Limits to Growth*?

7. Do the conclusions follow from the evidence?

8. What is the nature of the evidence?

9. Do you agree with these conclusions? If you agree, were you convinced by the arguments used in *The Limits to Growth* or had you reached the same conclusions independently?

10. Describe the policies advocated in *The Limits to Growth*.

11. Who will carry out these policies?

12. The authors of *The Limits to Growth* seem to imply that it will be impossible to deal with the five trends individually because man is unable to take correct action in relation to complex situations. Yet they advocate a plan for dealing with all five at once. Is this consistent?

13. The authors of *Limits to Growth* write that:

> ... the model is simply an attempt to bring together the large body of knowledge that already exists about cause-and-effect relationships among the five levels listed above and to express that knowledge in terms of interlocking feedback loops.

Are their conclusions, and the policies they advocate, in keeping with such a statement?

14. For publication in a national newspaper write an expanded summary of *The Limits to Growth*. Allow your own opinion of the book to become apparent.

15. In *The Limits to Growth* the executive committee of the Club of Rome stated that physical limits are 'further reduced by political, social and institutional constraints'. Discuss the validity of this view of social activity.

16. Are matters inevitably going to get worse?

In this, as in later chapters, teachers will need to read widely in the Additional Reading and beyond in order to be able to guide discussion of the important issues raised in these questions.

Chapter Two
Population

The explosive growth of the human population is the most significant terrestrial event of the past million millenia ... No geological event in a billion years — not the emergence of mighty mountain ranges, nor the submergence of entire sub-continents, nor the occurrence of periodic glacial ages — has posed a threat to terrestrial life comparable to that of human overpopulation.

Paul Ehrlich

The greatest possible impediment to more equal distribution of the world's resources is population growth.

The Limits to Growth

The size of a country's population and the proportion of the people in each age-group (its age-structure) is important for any government. The size of the population gives some idea of the quantities of food which have to be grown and imported and it is an important parameter in such calculations as the number of schools required or the number of teachers required in those schools. For example, the future demand for motorcars and motorways in the UK was worked out by extrapolating the curves of demand and population since 1945. The age-structure is one of the parameters required to establish the size of future population. Among others it is also necessary in the estimation of the money which will be required to pay old-age pensions.

An understanding of the size of future population will be based on the following areas of knowledge:
1. the size and rates of growth of present and future population;
2. the determinants of population growth;
3. methods and success of implementing population policy.

These might appear to be quite distinct areas. However, unless the numerical estimation of the size of future population is carried out by simple extrapolation of present data, such an estimation would include elements of the second category. At the same time, discussion of the determinants of population growth could include references to the methods of policy implementation.

1. Size of present and future population

In 1973, the authors of the massive United Nations report *The Determinants and Consequences of Population Trends* printed a table of population sizes from the distant past to the present entitled 'Conjectures of Historical Population Growth':

Date	Population (millions)	Average annual increase (%) since preceding date	Approximate number of years required for population to double at given rate
BC			
7000–6000	5–10		
AD			
1	200–400	0.0	
1650	470–545	0.0	
1750	629–961	0.4	173
1800	813–1125	0.4	173
1850	1128–1402	0.5	139
1900	1550–1762	0.5	139
1950	2486	0.8	86
1960	2982	1.8	38
1965	3289	2.0	35

The title itself suggests the tentative nature of the estimates. However it is generally agreed that there has been an exponential increase in population since 1600 AD.

The UN has also published estimates as to the size of world population in 2000 AD:

	Present (millions)	Low	Medium	High
Developed Countries	1090	1450	1450	1450
Developing Countries	2540	4520	5040	5650
Total	3630	5970	6490	7100

Whereas the estimates for developed or industrialized countries seem to have been estimated without nervousness, it should be noted that for the developing countries the variation between high and low estimates is over 1000 million. One of the factors used in calculating future population is the age-structure. If there is a large proportion of children the population can grow in size even if the birth rate drops. It should be noted that the authors of *The Limits to Growth* chose the highest figure for the year 2000.

How reliable are these forecasts? In answering this question it is helpful to introduce an historical perspective by examining (a) the accuracy of past forecasts and (b) the causes of population growth to date.

In 1978, Thomas Malthus an English clergyman wrote in his *Essay on the Principle of Population as it Effects the Future Improvement of Society*, that 'Population, when unchecked, increases in a geometrical ratio'. His research led him to define that ratio: without the checks of famine, disease, war, moral restraint and vice, a population would double every 25 years. He gave no exact quantitative extrapolations, but he did say that, 'In two centuries the population would be to the means of subsistence as 256 to 9'. (This estimate of growth rate would have forecast a British population of about 170 million by the year 1900).

Other historical forecasts were right for the wrong reasons. During the 1930s a USA forecast based on birth and death rates, agreed exactly with the subsequent census. But the result was not due to the predicted increase in birth and decrease in mortality; it came about through large-scale immigration from Europe which took place between the forecast and the census.

In his study of population forecasting including and since Malthus, Page has written that the 'basic data in demography are unsatisfactory — even if better than those found in other fields'. Even in Britain there is an error of about ¾ of 1% in the basic headcount, whereas in some countries errors of 10% or more are made. Besides which historical data are very scant and unreliable for most developing countries. He continued:

> The record in population forecasting is not impressive. Forecasts of the last century tended to be correct for several decades ahead, but this could hardly be attributed to forecasting expertise. Those of the inter-war period foresaw declines in the following few decades, whereas increases occurred. This is not a small quantitative quibble, it is qualitative error in forecasting the direction of the trend. The methodology of current extrapolative forecasts is not significantly different from those of the past, and so one does not have a sound basis for expecting present-day exercises to prove superior. The main problem lies, perhaps, in the implication of these techniques that population growth is an autonomous phenomenon, whereas it is clearly influenced by other natural and, to a greater extent, societal happenings. The conclusion of this paper is that it is impossible to know with certainty and accuracy a country's population over the long-term future.

But this does not mean that the present forecasts should be seen as too extreme and therefore to be ignored — particularly since the forecasts made during this century have generally underestimated future population sizes. It does mean that population forecasts should not be seen as inevitably predicting reality.

Finally in this section, we wish to mention one of the misconceptions that has been widely propagated about the present population growth rates in the developing countries: that because total populations are growing in some cases by large numbers, that birth rates are also increasing. Such statements ignore the small but definite indications of fall in birth rates in the two most populous countries in the world: India and China. At the same time, it ignores similar evidence for several countries of that other 'population explosion monster' Latin America: the sharp and persistent fall in Chile, Costa Rica, Cuba, and the low rates of increase in Uruguay and Argentina. A corollary of such a misconception is 'in those Latin American nations where growth rates are highest population control programs are not as yet even advocated'. This is also incorrect. In Mexico, which has had a high growth rate and which is the second most populous country in Latin America, not only are such programs 'advocated', but the government has at last begun to take them seriously. In fact out of the 66 countries (developed and developing) for which data are available, 56 report falling birth rates.

2. Determinants of population growth*

From antiquity men of knowledge and power have held opinions, based on political, military, social and economic considerations, about such issues as the most desirable number of people or the need to stimulate or retard population growth.

In Genesis, man is commanded to 'be fruitful and multiply and replenish the earth'. The teachings of Judaism followed this precept. Early medieval and Christian writers discussed population in moral and ethical terms. They reflected a conflict between the fear of depopulation and the need to accord with the celibate practices advocated by Paul: they condemned abortion, infanticide and child-exposure, yet glorified virginity and continence and frowned upon divorce and polygamy. Some writers saw population growth as the source of poverty, and pestilence, famine and war as nature's way of reducing excess population. The prevailing tendency however, was to favor population growth. The high mortality which was found everywhere and the constant threat of sudden depopulation through famine, epidemics and war, predisposed most writers to approve of a high birth rate. And behind this was an attitude of non-interference with pre-ordained processes which stemmed from a basic Christian understanding of the major determinant of population growth: Providence. God had decided and, therefore, would provide.

---

* The pre-agrarian phase has not been mentioned in this chapter. For a discussion of the first major demographic transition — from a hunting and gathering economy to an agrarian one — the reader is referred to the article by Dumond (1975).

The ideas of the philosophers of Ancient Greece dealt mainly with the population questions faced by a city state with a relatively small population. They considered the problem of population size not so much in economic terms, but more from the point of view of defence, security and government. Population should be self-sufficient; enough territory to supply its needs, but not too large as to make constitutional government impossible. A stable state was desired. In the case of under-population, Plato recommended rewards, advice or rebuke to the young in order to increase the birth rate, and, in the last resort, immigration. To remedy over-population he proposed birth control for large families and, if necessary, colonization. Aristotle considered that land could not be increased as fast as population could grow and concluded that an excessive number of people would breed poverty and social ills. Among the factors which could prevent an excessive population he mentioned child exposure and abortion.

In the Roman Empire, the views on population reflected the outlook of a society in which population was considered a source of power: the perspective of a great empire rather than a small city-state. They were less conscious than the Greeks of possible limits to population growth and more alert to its advantages for military and related purposes. The laws of Augustus, creating privileges for those married and having children and discriminating financially against those not married, aimed at raising the marriage and birth rates. It is nonetheless salutary to remember a comment made just over two centuries later by Tertullian when the Empire was no longer expanding: 'Pestilence, war and earth-quake have come to be regarded as a blessing to the nations, pruning the luxuriant growth of the human race'.

Throughout history, we repeatedly see the view that the largest population growth is the most desirable: a country or town needed men to defend its frontiers and men to work. For example, Sir Charles Davenport, the 17th century economist and political theorist of an expanding England, stated in *An Essay Upon Ways and Means of Supplying the War*:

> People are the real strength and riches of a country . . . 'Tis better that a people should want [lack] country than that a country should want people. No country can be truly accounted great and powerful by the extent of its territory or fertility of its climate, but by the multitude of its inhabitants.

The reasons for this digression into historical views of population growth are twofold:
(a) to show that many social and economic factors have been seen to affect theories of population growth — physical factors have not been seen as the only or principal determinants — policy decisions were also thought important;

(b) to suggest that in the main, for various reasons, population increase has been viewed as a Good Thing.

But to what extent did these early writers understand the links between the determinants and the resultant population growth. Did Augustus's Laws increase the size of population or, in a vigorous expanding economy, did the population grow regardless of laws? It seems that while many of the determinants were known, the precise relationships between cause and effect were unknown.

The 1973 UN Report mentioned above holds that no consistent population theory emerged before the late 18th century writings of Malthus. Since his time much has been written in this field. We will only discuss, briefly, Malthusian, Socialist and current theories as to the determinants of population growth.

(a) MALTHUS

Thomas Malthus's writings were touched off by discussions with his father who was an ardent supporter of optimistic theories of the nature of man. In his *Essay on the Principle of Population* (1798) he argued against Condorcet, who believed in the 'perfectability of the mass of mankind' and Godwin's allegations that the vices of mankind originated not inside man himself, but within human institutions. Malthus extended the previously proposed theory that 'population must always be kept down to the level of the means of subsistence' into 'the power of population is indefinitely greater than the power in the earth to produce subsistence for man'. From this it followed that 'the best directed exertions though they may alleviate can never remove the pressure of want' and therefore militate against any possibility of ever achieving an 'extraordinary improvement in society'. He also deduced that 'the principal and most permanent cause of poverty has little or no direct relation to forms of government or the unequal distribution of poverty. In the much revised and enlarged second and later editions of the *Essay* Malthus developed his theory further and examined at greater length the role of population as the basic cause of poverty.

His two fundamental laws are (i) population 'when unchecked increases in a geometrical ratio' (which we have seen before) and (ii) 'the means of subsistence could not possibly be made to increase faster than in an arithmetical ratio'. The combination of these results is a 'constant tendency in all animate life to increase beyond the nourishment prepared for it'. In a more formal manner he states his three propositions:

1. Population is necessarily limited by the means of subsistence.
2. Population invariably increases where the means of subsistence increases, unless prevented by some very powerful and obvious checks.

3. These checks, and the checks which suppress the superior power of population, and keep its effects on a level with the means of subsistence are all resolvable into moral restraint, vice and misery.

'Vice' consists not only of promiscuous intercourse, but of immoral acts (such as contraception, debauchery and infanticide); 'misery' is war, epidemics, famine and death from overcrowding and unhealthy living conditions; 'moral restraint' is restraint from marriage which is not followed by 'irregular gratifications' — the express intent of 'moral restraint' is not bringing life into being, because there is no prospect for life other than poverty.

Malthus's theories must be seen in the light of changing attitudes to the poor during the early 19th century. During the reign of Elizabeth the First an Act had provided that work should be found for those who had none. This had gradually changed into subsistence for the poor. Malthus, using the above propositions in conjunction with the laws of supply and demand, argued as follows: The Poor Laws encouraged more people to rely upon subsistence: the greater proportion of poor, on a higher income provided by the Poor Laws than if there were no Poor Laws, then produce still more poor by way of their children. Because there has been no increase in production only in population, the price of food rises, consequently lowering the actual wages of labourers outside the workhouses. The increase in the number of poor also forces the wages of the labourer down. This combined effect increases the number dependent upon relief which further aggravates the situation and threatens to reduce the whole country to dependence upon poor-relief. Besides, Malthus also believed that the poor had no 'natural right' to demand relief and had only themselves to blame for their poverty.

During the early 19th century, Malthus's theories were incorporated into the theories of what is known as the 'classical' school of economists.

While some writers have agreed that Malthus's effect on contemporary and ensuing events (as opposed to theories) was not very great and that none of his policies eventually succeeded in taking hold in the advanced industrialized societies, many others have seen that the *Essay* was welcomed by the ruling class and its effect was 'immediate and considerable . . . no more powerful contribution to the politicians outlook was made than that of the Malthusian theory'. It proved that society was not 'perfectible' and that it was impossible to 'remove the wants of the lower classes of society'. It was the Malthusian reform of the Poor Laws in 1834, which provided 'The chief and most permanent instrument of the policing of the working class'. It enforced the abolition of outdoor relief and replaced it by the grimmest workhouse conditions. Marx considered that 'the most open declaration of war by the bourgeosie upon the proletariat is Malthus's Law of Population and the New Poor Law framed in accordance with it'.

However, with the advance of the 19th century, the Malthusian population theory of the classical school was challenged by economic development, demographic facts, mathematical approaches, and the Socialists.

On the one hand economic progress and technological developments (particularly in agriculture) continued at such a rate that the increasing population was not seen to be suffering the greater deprivations that had previously been forecast. On the other hand, empirical demographic evidence showed that populations, although the means of subsistence were improving, were not increasing at the same rate as predicted by Malthus under such conditions. At the same time, it was increasingly felt that technological progress, the increase in human skills and natural productive wealth, and progressive social changes might counterbalance the tendency for population to press against the means of subsistence and thus produce diminishing returns. Many of the writers during this time accepted the Malthusian laws 'in principle' but thought that, through the continuing of changes recently brought about, the onset of diminishing returns could be delayed indefinitely or even offset completely.

Further, while some writers continued to be aware of the relationships between population growth and social and economic factors, others began to discuss the subject with little or no reference to social constraints. Progress in the natural and social sciences contributed not only to a better description and analysis of population phenomena but 'the conviction which emerged at that time that man and his actions were subject to certain well-defined laws, gave rise to the formulation of population theories in different fields'. It was argued that the theoretical basis for population growth could not be found in social or economic factors and institutions, but in natural biological, physical or chemical causes. The relevance of the mathematical theories which were proposed have been seriously questioned but the objective of relating population size only to physical factors still holds a certain fascination.

Besides the economic development and demographic factors which were contradicting Malthusian theories, the most serious theoretical opposition came from Socialist theories of population.

(b) SOCIALIST THEORIES ON POPULATION: MARX AND ENGELS

Marx saw the *Essay on Population* as a 'tract against the French Revolution and the contemporary ideas of reform in England' and Malthus as a 'shameless sycophant of the ruling classes' whose conclusions (including those of his economic work) were generally either in the interests of the ruling classes as a whole against the workers, or in the interests of the more reactionary sections of the ruling classes against the more progressive section. In addition to this he was guilty of the 'sin against science' — plagiarism. And he failed to investigate his premises fully.

In contrast to Malthus's 'abstract' principle of population, Marx held that there could be no natural and universal law of population; population was rather determined by the social and economic conditions prevailing in different societies. He insisted that each specific historic mode of production (which included a variety of social factors) had its own peculiar law of population, historically valid within its limits. In his view, 'an abstract law of population exists for plants and animals only, and only in so far as man has not interfered with them'.

In *Das Kapital* he outlined the population law 'peculiar to the capitalist mode of production'. 'Over-population' resulted from this mode of production, not from man's supposed biological proclivities. This 'surplus population' he termed the 'industrial reserve army'. It was fundamentally necessary to the workings of the capitalist economy. During boom periods extra capacity could be achieved by resorting to this army: 'The greater the social wealth, the functioning capital, the extent and energy of its growth, and therefore, also the absolute mass of the proletariat and the productiveness of labour, the greater is the industrial reserve army. The same causes which develop the expansive power of capital develop also the labour power at its disposal . . . This is the absolute general law of capital accumulation'.

Engels also considered that Malthus had looked at the population question from a superficial standpoint: the poor are not always with us, they are the product of a rotten social system. But he also considered that the question of food production had been incorrectly dealt with by Malthus. Ultimately, the land area is finite but (i) 'the labour power to be employed in this area increases together with the population' and (ii) 'the productivity of the land can be infinitely increased by the application of capital, labour and science . . . the progress of which is just as limitless and at least as rapid as that of population'.

(c) PRESENT THEORIES AS TO THE DETERMINANTS OF POPULATION GROWTH

Progress in demographic analysis, particularly in the study of fertility and mortality, has confirmed the necessity of formulating population theories not in terms of overall population growth but in terms of its main components — fertility and mortality.

At the same time there has been interest in the causes of world-wide population growth that has taken place since 1600 and in particular the way in which this has been tempered in the industrialized countries over the last 100 years. A theory has been developed which accounts for what has taken place: the theory of demographic transition. It is widely held that this theory has important implications for the population growth that is still taking place in the developing countries.

We will first examine the 'demographic transition' which accounts for the simultaneous behavior of fertility and mortality through time. Following that we will describe some of the factors which are now seen to influence fertility and mortality.

CURRENT THEORIES: DEMOGRAPHIC TRANSITION

From the 17th century there has been an unprecedented increase in world population. During the last 150 years another phenomenon has manifested itself: all the developed countries of the world have experienced an expanding and then a contracting rate of population growth. Several stages of growth have been identified:
(a) The high stationary stage characterized by high birth rates and high death rates;
(b) The early expanding stage, with high birth rates and high but decreasing mortality rates;
(c) The late expanding stage, with lower birth rates but more rapidly decreasing mortality;
(d) The low stationary stage, with low birth rates balanced by equally low mortality.
It has been argued that with the passage of time, other stages might be identified in certain countries such as relatively low and stable birth rates but sufficiently above mortality to permit minimal population increase or a declining state with birth rates below even a low mortality rate.

However, stages (a) to (d) are the ones through which all developed countries have passed. The explanation for this phenomenon of a 'demographic transition' is as follows:

The high birth rate has been seen as the result of both the parents' recognition of the high infant death rate and of the need to produce children as an insurance policy. High birth and death rates were the characteristic of life in the now developed world, at least since the development of agriculture, until the 17th and 18th centuries. The increase in population growth rate which took place during the 18th century was primarily caused by a fall in death rate. This fall in death rate has been variously attributed to the increase in effectiveness of medicine, the diffusion of public health measures, improved nutrition (through new methods of agriculture and distribution) and the higher standard of living which is given by the industrial way of life. It might be said that it followed from a combination of all four factors but at one time or another each has been seen as the major cause of the decrease in death rate and increase in population growth. However, the impact of better organization and improved medical knowledge and

27

care is most frequently seen as the major cause. (The allocation of responsibility to any of these factors has important implications as we will see when we consider methods of population control.) This phase of population growth is marked by birth rate not subject to calculation and a death rate already responding to human control.

Sometime after the fall in death rate the birth rate is seen to fall as a result of industrialization, urbanization, the growth of per capita income, and the increase of prudence.* Human beings have for the first time begun to calculate about the size of their families (without the need for making an allowance for deaths at birth) and have then been both willing to take advantage of smaller families and able to do so because of the widespread use of the techniques of birth control which vary from the various forms of contraception control through to abortion. The precise role of birth control as such is questioned. Although populations have continued to grow very substantially in absolute terms for several decades, thereafter the rate of growth declined until it reached the stage of low death and low birth rates. Thus, after a period of unprecedented growth, a new balance of births and deaths was achieved. At least in Western Europe and the United States of America the pre-demographic transition equilibrium with birth rate and death rates in excess of 30 per thousand, had been replaced by an equilibrium with both rates under 15 per thousand.

The major cause underlying the demographic transition has been seen as the growth of industrialization. As the authors of *The Limits to Growth* state:

> As it stands (the relationship between industrial output and desired birth rate) simply reflects the historical behaviour of human society. Wherever economic development has taken place, birth rates have fallen. When industrialization has not occurred, birth rates have remained high.

The present situation in the third world is seen as the result of 'exporting death control' to these countries. The solution is seen by many to lie in economic development.

However, it has been argued that since the transition theory is linked to the experience of Western countries, whose historical trends were by themselves far from uniform, it is unlikely that it provides more than vague suggestions about factors which may determine growth in other countries. Further, it is not a theory but a description of historical events that have occurred in the developed countries with some

* *See* Davis (1973) for a discussion of the fact that in many urban areas of Europe the decline in the birth rate actually anticipated the decline in the death rate.

irregularity. It has suggested certain major complexes of factors which presumably influence the components of population growth. But it is questioned whether these complexes are sufficiently well defined to permit a system of logically consistent and explicit relationships that provide a basis for building a model, such as *The Limits to Growth*. The cause and effect link between industrialization and a fall in birth rate is, for example, thrown into doubt by the fact that in Sweden and France, the fall in birth rate *preceded* industrialization. Other problems will be raised during the discussion of fertility and mortality taken separately. Here it is sufficient to ask to what extent the demographic transition has been understood in the context of the countries where it took place. And to what extent that understanding merits its acceptance as a predictive explanation of future developments in developing countries.

CURRENT THEORIES: FERTILITY AND MORTALITY

As mentioned above one of the means of investigating the determinants of population growth is to identify rigorously the factors separately affecting fertility and mortality. Forecasting then involves the assessment of how these variables act in concert with one another.

Birth Rates. Fertility can be defined as 'actual reproductive performance'. There are wide variations in concept and methodology which affect different authors' presentation of the various factors affecting fertility. The United Nations report mentioned earlier isolates four categories:
1. Fundamental, underlying factors relating to the economic and social structure.
2. Cultural factors.
3. Intermediate factors: customs and practices.
4. Intermediate factors: physiological.
'Intermediate' factors have been so named because they constitute the variables ". . . through which any of the social factors influencing the level of fertility must operate". The physiological subset are: maximum possible biological fertility rates (i.e. fecundity), age limits to the reproductive period, post-partum sterility, and involuntary fetal mortality and other forms of sterility and sub-fecundity.

The customs and practices affecting fertility are: age of entry into sexual unions; age at marriage; permanent celibacy; amount of reproductive period spent after or between unions; voluntary abstinence (social taboos on sexual intercourse); fetal mortality from voluntary causes (abortion); voluntary infecundity (sterilization) and the use or non-use of contraception.

The UN authors emphasize that each of the intermediate variables is a variable in the sense that 'it can operate either to reduce or enhance fertility'. Consequently, the level of fertility of a population results

29

from the joint effect of (the values of) all eleven variables. They continue:

> Further, a population, even though it may have a high fertility value on some variables, for example, universal marriage at an early age, may none the less have a low or moderate fertility level because of low fertility values on other variables, such as the use of contraceptives or recourse to abortion (voluntary fetal mortality). Two populations may have approximately the same level of fertility despite very different values of all or most of the intermediate variables.

By cultural factors they refer broadly to all motivational aspects of reproductive behavior, although principally to the 'institutionalized norms and values of a society by which individuals are guided in their actions relating to the number of children they have'. A study of the social norms which form around the institution of the large family found that they were supported by 'public opinion, moral canons, the rules of marriage and, lastly, the precepts of religion, which of course did not create the traditions but only strengthened established national customs'. These cultural values have also been defined as 'attitudes and interests which are, in part, engendered by a particular social structure and which in turn motivate and direct the activities of the individuals who form a society'.

This motivational factor is apparently not always taken into account in writings on factors affecting fertility. However, many writers believe that the decline of fertility in European society involved profound changes in motivation. But, as there is a scarcity of data relating to the decline of fertility in those countries where fertility has already fallen to low or moderate levels 'views about how much of a modification in motivation occurred are of necessity largely conjectural'.

While acknowledging the importance of motivation, the UN authors, in discussing the modern movement of family limitation in the United Kingdom, state 'although there is evidence that a latent desire for smaller families existed before that time', it was only under the cumulative impact of '. . . the profound (social and economic) changes that were taking place in the outlook and ways of living of the people . . .' that the psychological barriers to birth control were broken down. It is to these social and economic factors that we now turn.

'Any selection of underlying factors affecting fertility trends is necessarily of arbitrary nature and in this respect reflects the lack of agreement and even confusion found in the literature'. The economic and social factors selected for review by the authors of the United Nations report were: (a) family functions and structure, (b) relationships between mortality and fertility (c) rising levels of living and increased costs of children's upbringing (d) levels of education (e) social mobility (f) urbanization, and (g) industrialization.

In discussing the effect of these factors upon the decline of fertility in the industrialized countries the authors state that attempts to associate the decline with a particular factor have not proved satisfactory:

> Fertility fell in Spain, Bulgaria and other Southern and Eastern European countries when mortality was still very high, in many countries rural fertility declined as early and as much as urban fertility; in some countries industrialization was far advanced before marital fertility fell, in others a major decline preceded substantial industrialization . . . In European national experience, the only factor apparently always changing at the same time that fertility declined was literacy, but the onset of fertility decline has no consistent relationship with the proportion literate at the time.

In the light of the discussion on the theory of demographic transition and fertility, you are now encouraged to consider the confidence with which the authors of *The Limits to Growth* state 'the major effect of rising GNP is on the desired birth rate'.

Death Rates. The UN report states 'the complicated interplay of various biological, economic, social and cultural factors has an impact on the health of individuals and hence on the mortality levels of populations'. They examine the demographic, economic, social and cultural factors which affect mortality. The sex and age structure of the population are the main demographic factors considered, since the crude death rate is influenced by the proportion of aged persons in the population and by the ratio between sexes, males generally having higher mortality than females in modern times (in the developed countries). The economic and social factors which influence the level of mortality are numerous and of considerable complexity; they include, for example, occupation, educational level, nutritional standards, living conditions, sanitation, public health services, medical services and the general level of living. Available statistics make it possible to draw inferences regarding the factors which determine the rates. 'Because those factors are mutually interdependent, however, a satisfactory quantitative estimate of the influence of any one factor is very difficult to obtain'.

Many authors attribute the fall in death rate over the last 200 years as predominantly due to two factors: increase in effectiveness of medicine, and improvement in sanitary conditions in urban areas (public health). The UN report states:

> Whatever the broad categories used for analysis, it is clear that underlying the multitude of individual factors responsible for the reductions in mortality have been the more or less continuous economic advances resulting from the so-called agricultural and

31

industrial revolutions; this progress made possible the development and applications in technology, public health, sanitation
and medicine which were crucial for substantial mortality decline.

However, recent workers, some of whom are mentioned in the UN
report, have stated quite adamantly that such an emphasis is misplaced.
They have argued that the improvements in economic conditions
resulted in better nutritional standards, and that this was the main
cause of the substantial fall in tuberculosis mortality in England and
Wales during the second half of the 19th century, and was probably a
factor, although to a lesser extent, in the decline of the mortality from
typhus.

Elsewhere, Porter has recorded the combined death rate for children
under 15 from scarlet fever, diphtheria, whooping cough and measles
from 1860—1965. 'Nearly 90 per cent of the total decline in the death
rate over this period had occurred before the introduction of antibiotics
and widespread immunization against diphtheria'. Since nearly half of
the decline in mortality in the second half of the 19th century was in
the decline of deaths attributed to tuberculosis and a fifth in the
decline of deaths attributed to scarlet fever, it has been argued that
the major determinants of health are nutrition and the general raising
of living standards, as opposed to medicine and sanitary conditions.
McKeown in *The Modern Rise of Population* has identified the increase
in food supplies as the main factor in mortality decline. In relation to
the debate about mortality decline in the third world, Powles (1977)
has concluded:

1. The hypotheses that mortality decline in the Third World has been
   predominantly due to either disease control measures or material
   betterment do not deserve to be retained.
2. This is not to deny that the achievement of a more favorable balance
   between numbers and food supplies is the single most important
   factor in the long term.
3. The most critical determinants of an accelerated mortality decline,
   at least through the middle ranges of mortality, are social modernization and effective public administration. These seem to be
   important in their own right and as facilitators of other determinants.

While such conclusions are controversial, they are very important in
the discussion of methods of implementation of population policies. It
is to these that we now turn.

3. Methods of implementing population policies

We have examined the forecasts of the size of future population, and
the determinants of population growth and have noted the effect of
social and economic factors upon both population and population

policy. It has been shown that the inter-relationships between the various factors affecting population growth are incompletely understood. As the UN report states:

> despite the better insight and understanding they have provided, none of the approaches has as yet produced a completely accepted theory of population.

And therefore, the difficulty for policy makers and forecasters is knowing the outcome of their policies and forecasts with any degree of accuracy. This dilemma may be illustrated by two examples. Firstly, it is questioned whether the 'demographic transition' which occurred in the developed countries will take place in the developing countries, and thus limit population growth. Even if it does, it is questioned whether the concept of economic growth implied in the 'theory of demographic transition' necessarily entails systems of advanced industrialization and urbanization.

Secondly, the debate as to whether the prime cause of the fall in death rate during the 19th century was the improvement of medicine, sanitation, nutrition or the general raising of standards of living has important implications for the third world. If medicine and sanitary conditions were the major determinants of health, then a government should obviously encourage both to its utmost by training doctors, engineers, builders and institutions. But if nutrition and the raising of living standards were the major determinants then its efforts should be focused in another direction.

One of the most popular methods to achieve the objective set by a population policy has been birth control. In the long run some form of birth control is essential in order to aid the achievement and maintenance of an adequate level of food per capita. The questions raised by birth control are many and varied. It is not my intention to pursue them here but only to mention in passing that they involve considerations of an ethical, administrative, scientific, technological, sociological, political and financial nature.

4. Topical attitudes and policies towards population

We have examined the estimates of present and future populations, the determinants of growth and the methods of implementing population policies. Now we will briefly examine some of the topical attitudes at work today that might affect population policies. From our previous discussion of determinants and methods we should be in a position to assess the viability of these attitudes and policies.

People are pollution asserts Paul Ehrlich in his provocatively titled book *The Population Bomb*. He is not alone, J. K. Brierly in *Biology and the Social Crisis* states 'The most urgent problem is that of population, for unchecked fertility is the root of most of the social, economic and health problems the world is facing', and mentions 'as a direct result of population pressure . . .' urbanization and traffic problems, war, political instabilities, infant mortalities and the loss of many wild flower and insect species, and the habitats of many mammals and birds. And we have seen the opinion of the authors of *The Limits to Growth* that 'the greatest possible impediment to more equal distribution of the world's resources is population growth'. It seems to be the dominant view.

These attitudes are reflected by governments of many countries. Nixon proclaimed to Congress (18 July 1969): 'one of the most serious challenges to human destiny in the last third of this century will be the growth of population . . . many of our present social problems may be related to the fact that we have had only 50 years in which to accommodate to the second hundred million Americans'. Singapore is currently conducting what may be the world's most intensive population control program, including such moves as strong financial penalties against having children. In 1970, the Prime Minister of Ghana, launching his country's family planning program, justified it thus: 'The present rate of growth increases our population by 5000 people every week . . . In simple terms it means that as a nation, we are increasing in number faster than we can build schools to educate our youth, faster than we can construct hospitals to cater for the health needs of the people, and faster than we can develop our economy to provide jobs for the more than 140,000 new workers who enter our labour force each year'.

However, there are those who object to the onus for pollution, decimation of the species, and over-use of resources, being laid in the lap of the individual, and in particular, the individual of the third world. These objections stem from various vantage points.

Geoffrey Hawthorn in *Population Policy: A Modern Delusion* argues that certain 'qualities of life' [his quotation marks] are felt to be threatened, and a culprit is needed. 'Hence the attention to population growth'. He considers this attention doubly misleading: population control would change few things (unless you imagine unrealistic rates of change), and, moreover, focusing attention on population diverts it away from important issues like the social responsibility of industry or priorities in social policy. Indeed, some economists have denied that a high rate of population growth necessarily brings with it economic problems. 'The economic effects of a high rate of population growth', the economist Kuznets writes of the developing countries, 'would not constitute a major obstacle to an increase in per capita production'.

Some socialist writers, following Marx, see that the fault lies not with the individual, but in the social system. They can certainly point to Cuba and China. Who talks of the starving millions of China any more?

Others disagree with those who predict only adverse effects from population growth, on the grounds that such opinions are dangerous in themselves. They refer to the consequences of Hitler's policies regarding 'Lebensraum' and the growth of the Jewish population, and point to present policies in South Africa where one fifth of the population is encouraged to procreate for the 'good of the nation', whereas four fifths of the population are discouraged from such activities, also for the 'good of the nation'.

Finally, Passmore has written 'To surrender our freedom, to abandon all respect for persons, in the name of control over population growth is to make sacrifices which our proper concern for posterity cannot justify'. The attitude that population growth itself is not the major problem is reflected at government level. The demographic problem, according to a delegate from the Soviet Union to the United Nations Population Commission of 1963, is 'not a real one'. More recently, a Mexican government official: 'High birth rates are a problem of developing countries. There is no case of a high birth rate in an industrialized nation. Our real problem is, therefore, not the birth rate, but rather the poverty, illiteracy, unemployment and low productivity that produces it. And the solution is not to force down the birth rate artificially, but to improve the standard of living'. (Nevertheless, Mexico has, in fact, recently changed its official views, and is now actively engaged in family planning activities.)

It must be stressed, however, that it is not only Socialists or economic optimists who think this way. Few Catholic countries have active policies to reduce population – some like France and Brazil, actively promote growth (dislike of birth control is not their only argument in favor of population growth). Pope Pius VI told the UN General Assembly in 1965 'You must strive to multiply bread so that it suffices for the tables of mankind, and not, rather favor an artificial control of birth, which would be irrational, in order to diminish the number of guests at the banquet of life'.

In the following chapter we will examine what is entailed by the Pope's exhortation to 'multiply bread'.

Reading

ESSENTIAL

2.1   Meadows *et al.* (1972). (*ref. 1.1*), Chapter 1 and pp. 109–117.
2.2   Page, R. W. 'The Population Sub-system', Chapter 4 in Cole *et al.* (1973) (*ref. 1.3*), pp. 43–55.
2.3   Page, R. W., 'Population Forecasting', Chapter 11 in Cole *et al.* (1973) (*ref. 1.3*), pp. 159–174.
2.4   Passmore, John, *Man's Responsibility for Nature.* Duckworth, 1974. Chapter 6, 'Multiplication', pp. 127–170.

ADDITIONAL

2.5 Beckmann, Petr, *Eco hysterics and the technophobes.* The Golem Press, 1973. Chapter 2 'The Population Exploders', pp. 31–63. An optimistic approach to the population question.

2.6 Borrie, W. D., *The Growth and Control of World Population.* Weidenfeld, 1970.

2.7 Clark, Colin, *Population Growth and Land Use.* Macmillan, 1967.

2.8 Commoner (1972) (*ref. 1.4*), pp. 211–215, 232–249, 293–300.

2.9 Clarke, Arthur, *Profiles of the Future.* Harper & Row, 1962.

2.10 Davis, K., 'Cities and Mortality', *Proceedings of the International Population Conference.* Liege, 1973. International Union for the Scientific Study of Population, Liege, 1973, Vol. 3 , pp. 259–281.

2.11 Dumond, D., 'The limitations of human population: a natural history'. *Science* (1975) **187**, pp. 713–721.
Discusses the first major demographic transition – from a hunting and gathering economy to an agrarian one – and the second major transition – from an agrarian to an industrial economy.

2.12 Ehrlich (1971). (*ref. 1.6*).
According to Ehrlich, people are the problem.

2.13 Ehrlich, Paul and Ehrlich, Anne, *Population, Resources, Environment: Issues in Human Ecology.* W. H. Freeman, 1970.

2.14 Eyer, J., 'Prosperity as a cause of death', *International Journal of Health Services* (1977) 7, pp. 125–150.

2.15 Habakkuk, H. J., *Population Growth and Economic Development since 1750.* Leicester University Press, 1971.
The theory of 'Demographic Transition' and its critics.

2.16 Hardin, Garrett, 'The Tragedy of the Commons'. In John Barr (ed.), *The Environmental Handbook.* Pan Paperback, 1971.

2.17 Malthus, Thomas, *Essay on the Principle of Population* (ed. Himmelfarb). Modern Library, 1960.

2.18 Meek, R. L., *Marx and Engels on Malthus.* Lawrence and Wishart, 1953.

2.19 McKeown, T., *The Modern Rise of Population.* Arnold, 1976.
A good reference on the transition from agrarian to industrial demography. A small book that summarizes McKeown's work.

2.20 Powles, J., 'Reasons for the modern decline in mortality in the Third World – the apparent importance of social modernization'. In N. Hicks (ed.), ANZSERCH (Australian and New Zealand Society for Epidemology and Community Health). *Proceedings of the annual meeting 1976.* ANZSERCH, 1977.

2.21 United Nations Department of Economic and Social Affairs, *The Determinants and Consequences of Population Trends Vol 1.* UN, 1973.
An excellent survey of the issues.

2.22 United Nations Department of Economic and Social Affairs, *World Population Prospects as Assessed in 1963.* UN, 1966.

2.23 United Nations Department of Economic and Social Affairs, *World Population Prospects Assessed in 1968.* UN, 1973.

2.24 United Nations Department of Economic and Social Affairs, *The Population Debate — Dimensions and Perspectives.* Papers of the World Population Conference, Bucharest, 1974, Vol. 1 and 2. UN, 1975.

2.25 Cole, Sam and Miles, Ian, 'Assumptions and Methods: Population, Economic Development, Modelling and Technical Change'. Chapter 3 in Freeman & Jahoda (eds.), 1978 *(ref. 1.8).*

2.26 *Bulletin of the Atomic Scientists,* **XXX,** (6), June 1974. Whole issue on population.

2.27 'The human population', *Scientific American,* **231,** (3), Sept. 1974, (whole issue).

2.28 Brown, L. R., 'The population problem in 22 dimensions', *Futurist,* **10,** Oct. 1976, pp. 238–45.

2.29 Djerassi, Carl, 'The Chinese achievement in fertility control', *Bulletin of the Atomic Scientists,* **XXX,** (6), June 1974.

2.30 Hardin, G., 'The case against helping the poor', *Psychology Today,* Sept. 1974.

2.31 Holdren, J. P. and Ehrlich, P. R., 'Human population not the global environment', *American Scientist,* **62,** (3), May–June 1974, pp. 282–292.

2.32 Reddaway, W. B., 'The economic consequences of zero population growth', *Lloyd Bank Review,* No. 124, Apr. 1977, pp. 14–30.

2.33 *The Journal of Development Studies,* **14,** (4), July 1978. Special issue on population and development.

Points for discussion or essays

1. No one denies that increase in population is an issue affecting many people. Most writers agree that it is a problem. Several questions arise out of such a view:
   (a) Is population growth the most important problem facing the world today? If so, why?
   (b) If it is a major problem should we attempt to control population growth? *(ref. 2.4).*
   (c) How should population growth be controlled? *(ref. 2.4).* Discuss the proposals which have been suggested for the control of population growth.
2. Describe and discuss present attitudes to population growth.

Discuss present policies towards population and their anticipated effect upon population growth. (*refs. 2.4, 2.13*).
3. Discuss the relation between population theory and society. (*refs. 2.15, 2.18, 2.19*).
4. Discuss the determinants of population growth. (*Ref. 2.21*).
5. Discuss the theory of 'demographic transition' and its current application. (*refs. 2.15, 2.19*).
6. On pp. 26–31 of *ref. 2.13* the age distributions of five different countries (Mauritius, United Kingdom, India, Japan, USA) are given. Discuss the meaning of the different curves obtained for each country.
7. Discuss the accuracy of population statistics. (*ref. 2.3*).
8. It has been observed that when people have a choice they have fewer children. Equally that in poor societies people often have many children. Discuss the validity of both observations in relation to two industrialized and two developing countries.

(Further questions concerning the relation between (a) food and population and (b) natural resources and population may be found at the ends of Chapters 3 and 4.

Questions related to *The Limits to Growth*

1. 'The two key problems for the population sub-model relate to the paucity of real world knowledge of population dynamics, and the extent to which population growth is determined by matters of a policy nature as well as a physical nature'. Discuss Page's reasons for reaching these conclusions. (*ref. 2.2*).
2. Discuss the role of policies related to population growth in *The Limits to Growth*.
3. 'The overall behavior of the world model is relatively insensitive to changes in the output of the population sub-system'. In what ways might this conclusion affect those reached in *The Limits to Growth*? (*ref. 2.2*).
4. Discuss the relation between Industrial Output per capita and Desired Total Fertility. The model considers that this is the major determinant of fertility. Is this fully justifiable?

Chapter Three
Food

> History records more acute shortages in individual countries, but it is doubtful whether such a critical food situation has been so world-wide.
> (Main Report of 1974 World Food Conference)

Resources are the means by which people physically sustain themselves and their man-made environment. We will be considering food in this chapter and mineral and non-renewable resources in the next.

National leaders have encouraged food production for the following different reasons:

1. National self-sufficiency: a concern originating from the vulnerability of a nation in times of war;
2. Reducing imports;
3. Benefits for the farm population: higher incomes, stable prices and expanded investment opportunities;
4. Benefits for consumers: assured supply at stable and reasonable prices.

However, these reasons seem somewhat bland by comparison with the many alarming estimates of the present food situation. For example, Georg Borgstrom has written:

> Basically there are not many oases left in a vast, almost world-wide network of slums; about 450 million well fed people living in comparative luxury . . . as against 2400 million undernourished, malnourished, and in other ways deficiently fed and generally poor.

By malnourished is meant the individual is not receiving enough food to lead a healthy life. Estimates of the numbers of people actually starving to death each year start at 10 to 15 million — this number is felt to be very low as it does not include those killed by diseases caused by starvation or by diseases to which starvation has made the body vulnerable by eroding its natural resistance. The situation has been seen by some as chronic and with population increasing all the time it is widely anticipated that it can only get worse. If the world is not capable of adequately feeding its present population of 3.6 billion, then there is surely little hope of feeding the population expected by the 2000. What are the prospects of feeding the anticipated population?

Broadly speaking, three types of answer have been given to this question:

1. Total world food production may or may not be adequate for the present population. But the potential is much greater than the present figures show; it will be possible to feed the growing population.
2. Total world food production is not adequate to feed the present population. It will not be possible to increase food production on a sufficient scale, or at a sufficient speed, to feed the rapidly doubling population.
3. While acknowledging the need to increase food production by whatever means are available, the third answer to the question sees political factors as of overriding importance. The difficulties of feeding both the present and future populations are seen to lie in the political roots of poverty which create a situation of ineffective demand for the means to produce and pay for food. Also the political divisions between the nations of the world are seen to impede the rational production and distribution of food.

Each of these answers has different implications for government policies in relation to food. For example, in the case of (1): increase food production by whatever means and improve the efficiency of the chain of distribution on a national and international scale. In the case of (2): decrease the size of population and encourage national self sufficiency, and for (3): tackle the question of the political roots of poverty at the same time as increasing the production and supply of food.

The first two types of answer to the question (What are the prospects of feeding the anticipated population?) may be seen to stem from what McLean and Hopkins have called 'the aggregate approach' to food production. In essence, the aggregate approach — particularly the optimism implied in the first answer — has been the dominant one since the Second World War. Many governments throughout the world and international institutions such as FAO have adopted policies aimed at increasing aggregate national food supplies and the creation of world food surpluses that can be shipped to wherever they are needed.

During the late sixties some experts claimed that despite (a) the massive increase in the productivity of the industrialized countries (b) the massive food aid programs and (c) the massive campaigns to raise productivity throughout the developing world — despite all these measures, world food production was not able to stay ahead of population growth, and starvation was increasing. With this realization many experts began to provide the second answer to the question 'What are the prospects . . . ?': world famine.

The 1974 World Food Conference saw a kind of compromise between these two answers which stem from the aggregated approach to food production (see the quote at the head of this chapter). It was argued that nations should no longer rely upon the creation of storable world surpluses but should aim for greater self-sufficiency through greater national production and more efficient methods of food distribution within each country. Instead of world surpluses, national surpluses are advocated as the best defence against world famine.

The third answer — tackle the roots of poverty and production — has recently begun to be advocated by some experts. At a conference in Bucharest it seemed to be acknowledged as relevant by representatives of countries in Eastern Europe and the third world as well as some Catholic countries. However, as yet it is not as widely recognized as either of the other two answers which concentrate on the quantity of food produced.

We will first examine the arguments of those who have looked at the world food problem on an aggregated production basis — and summarize briefly the optimistic and pessimistic arguments which prevail in the debate on this subject. Later we will turn to the arguments of those who advocate the third answer to the problem of feeding future populations.

Increasing world food production

The basic factors affecting food production are the amount and quality of land, the climate, the methods used to farm it, and the possibilities of new forms of synthetic foods. Pirie has written that the improvement of agriculture has always depended on two factors: the systematization and application of old experience and the acquisition of new knowledge. Increasing the area farmed, and the methods used during farming may be seen as the former, whereas possible new research and development including synthetic foods and the modification of climate represent the latter.

THE AREA FARMED

Estimates of the amount of land that potentially is arable vary from 20% to 30% of the earth's surface. There is some agreement that about 10% of it is actually farmed and that this land is the most suitable for farming and the most accessible. Although the Malthusian prediction was foiled by the opening up of new farm land in the Americas, Australia and Siberia, it is not expected that new land of similar potential will be discovered in the future. Until recently the largest readily exploitable land was the 33 million acres withheld from agriculture in the USA. This has now been brought into use.

Although the example of the Netherlands is often quoted as an example of the benefits of land reclamation, it must be recognized that the Netherlands represents a process that has been creeping forward over the last three centuries — it is no quick alternative and it is very expensive. 'We cannot look forward to any large increase in the farmed area in the Temperate Zone and should concentrate instead of using the area we have more efficiently'. It has been suggested that the simplest improvement in the older countries would be the conversion of small fields into larger ones: the hedge round a five acre field occupies half an acre.

In the cold lands north of the Temperate Zone the massive use of glasshouses has been advocated as a method of increasing the area used. The prospect of opening up new farming areas in the hot arid regions of the world has also been examined. These areas are estimated at between 23 and 60% of the earth's land surface depending upon the criteria of aridity used. But either way their sheer size presents an alluring prospect if ways could be found to overcome their dryness. These are usually considered in terms of irrigation although more dramatic means such as artificial alteration of climate and the towing of icebergs from Antarctica to the Middle East, have received widespread publicity.

The 'wet tropics' have, however, a much more uniform climate than the so-called Temperate Zone and their potential productivity is much greater than that of any other area that remains unexploited. The forested humid tropics make up 40% of the total area of Africa and 42% of South America. Nonetheless there is reason to think that a fundamental piece of knowledge about agriculture in the wet tropics is missing. We do not know what to grow.

Apparently the indigenous foods — tapioca, yams, bananas, sugar-cane, sago, breadfruit, etc. — are excellent sources of carbohydrate but it is not possible to obtain an adequate supply of protein from these plants. Seed bearing plants which produce vegetable protein for the peoples of the Temperate Zone, need a dry spell for ripening. In hot climates where it rains every day, they rot. Thus, only if there are adequate fish and animal species is there a protein source. At the same time if the land is cleared of its forest cover and treated in the same way as land in the Temperate Zone, leaching occurs and the land erodes. The basic problem is that intensive farming methods developed for the Temperate Zone do not work in the tropics. Until nutritionally valuable crops that can be grown in the tropics are developed, or discovered, and new farming methods suitable to the particular environment are found, it will not be possible to increase the area of farm land in the wet tropics.

The general conclusions reached after discussion of the above difficulties are that opening up new land for farming will be difficult. But there are distinct differences in the estimates of cost. The authors of *The Limits to Growth* assume that the cost of opening new land will be the average of the costs for developing new land throughout the world which varies from the $5275 p.a. in the USA to $215 in poor countries the average being $1150. This is one of the key assumptions in their model. The assumption is denied by Marstrand and Pavitt in their chapter of *Thinking about the Future*. They raise two objections.

Firstly, the empirical data used to ascertain development costs are suspect, particularly in the upper range of development costs. Secondly, they show that the method used to calculate development costs implicitly assumes that agricultural investment decisions will continue to be made on a national basis i.e. it assumes political rather than physical limits. This method contradicts the model's assumption of perfect mobility of capital and labor on a world scale. If the model's assumptions were maintained (which would be in accordance with the proclaimed intention of examining physical limits) then to increase the area farmed in the cheapest way, one would start by investing in those areas in the world with the lowest development costs. Do such regions exist on a large scale? About 50% of the world's potentially arable land is at present under cultivation. In the densely populated continents of Europe and S.E. Asia, the percentage is over 80; in North America and the USSR it is between 50 and 60; but in Africa, Australasia and South America it is around 15 to 20. Therefore there are large regions in the world which could be developed at costs far below the world average. The degree to which investment capital is drained off in order to achieve a given agricultural output depends very much on whether these lands are developed before the more costly ones. If there were a rational use of agricultural resources the development costs would be much lower than those used in the *Limits to Growth* model.

However because political boundaries exist which tend to limit such a rational use of the remaining arable land, physical limits to agricultural production might well be approached in certain densely populated regions, for example S.E. Asia. Thus, whereas Ehrlich and the MIT authors forecast world famine, consideration of the world on a *disaggregated* basis does lead to anticipation of localized famines.

METHODS USED TO INCREASE PRODUCTIVITY

We have seen that at the end of the eighteenth century Malthus predicted disastrous consequences because population increased geometrically whereas agricultural production could only increase arithmetically. The pessimistic forecast was partly confounded by the great increases in productivity which were brought about by the introduction of new farming methods: improved crop rotation and mechanization. Later the introduction of fertilizers and pesticides resulted in further substantial increases.

Malthus also predicted that each increase in food production would require a greater increase in labor, equipment and finance: this is known as the law of diminishing returns. As with the assumption that agricultural production could only increase arithmetically it has not yet been proven true. In this respect, Engels predicted:

The town industry as it is today will be able to spare people enough to give agriculture quite other forces than it has had up to now; science will also then at last be applied to agriculture on a large scale and with the same consistency as in industry.

In the USA, for example, the percentage of people employed in agriculture has shrunk from ninety in 1790, to seven today (only about 3.2% in England and Wales). The improvements in labor productivity have continued into the twentieth century. Each farmer now produces six times as much as in 1920, and the average yield per acre has nearly doubled.

The methods by which productivity improvements have been made are
(a) Increased mechanization;
(b) Improved crop rotation procedures;
(c) Introduction of fertilizers;
(d) Introduction of pesticides;
(e) Increased irrigation;
(f) Introduction of new food species. Every major food plant, except for rice, is now grown more extensively in some country into which it has been introduced than in its country of origin.
(g) Improved marketing and distribution of food.

It is envisaged that vast increases in production will be obtained by the application of this knowledge to the lands in the developing countries which, by and large, have not yet been the object of these new farming practices. But only 7% of the lands in the poorer parts of the world are farmed by methods similar to those used in Western Europe. It would seem absurd to conclude that the remaining 93% could not experience the increases in productivity which have taken place over the last 150 years. The yields of maize in the USA and rice in Japan are three times what they are in India. It is possible that sufficient food for the present world population would be produced if the productivity of the developing countries could be increased as much as it has been increased in the industrialized countries. It should be stressed that these methods do not involve techniques yet to be discovered in the laboratory. They involve the transfer of methods already tried and tested in the fields of the industrialized countries, to those of the developing countries. However these methods often depend on a high input of energy.

Recently high yield varieties of grain were discovered as a result of an intensive research program. The increases in production which were obtained in certain areas by the application of new farming methods to the growing of these high yield varieties were expected to be duplicated throughout the third world: 'The Green Revolution'.

Against such an assessment of the possibilities for increased world food production — which is, essentially, that the increases already achieved in the industrialized countries can be repeated throughout the world — we find the following array of arguments:

(a) Malthusian law of diminishing returns to agricultural investment (one of the assumptions in *The Limits to Growth*), an argument which is more applicable to developed than to under-developed countries.
(b) Aggregate production sufficient — the FAO estimates that the average calories needed (per capita per day) are 2354 and that 2420 are available at the market level — but there is difficulty ensuring that the surplus from one area arrives at the place where it is needed: the inefficiency and inequity arise from the chain of distribution, and the differences in purchasing power.
(c) Aggregate production of calories sufficient but a protein deficiency of chronic proportions.
(d) The relative failure of the Green Revolution:
    (i) The new strains are fussy and need particularly careful attention throughout their growing life, i.e. difficulties of training people to use them,
    (ii) The pesticides and fertilizers used to grow these new crops are expensive (and energy dependent);
    (iii) The crucial importance of correct quantities of water at the right time, i.e. vulnerability to climatic variation and dependence upon good irrigation;
    (iv) The technologies are difficult to acquire — difficult to get people to adopt new methods;
    (v) New pests.
The combination of the above has meant that the new high yield varieties have in fact only been utilized by the large landowners who are already rich — it has widened disparities between the rich and poor.
(e) Very little known of tropical crops — need for further research (this has been discussed above).
(f) Reliance by the third world upon the charity of USA surpluses saps initiative and breeds a subject race.
(g) Certain systems of land tenure inhibit the adoption of modern methods. For example, owners may demand more rent if the land is more productive.

The following arguments are also used at times:

(h) Monoculture is inherently bad and should be avoided: disruption of ecology, unstable in itself, needs massive artificial inputs to sustain it and is susceptible to climatic changes and seasonal fluctuations.
(i) The difficulties of introducing change into agricultural communities. This has been explicitly denied in relation to the European farming communities. In relation to the third world it is widely recognized that there can be difficulties in introducing change — in both the methods of farming and the willingness to eat the crop (food tastes). The prime example is always the sacred cows of India which are not

viewed as a food resource but as one of the sections of society for which food must be grown. On the one hand, both the difficulty of introducing new farming methods and of changing food tastes have been challenged. On the other, in the context of *The Limits to Growth* debate, it should be remembered that these represent social constraints, not absolute physical limits to the quantities of food that can be grown, but nevertheless *real* constraints.

SYNTHETIC FOODS AND CLIMATE MODIFICATIONS

We have seen that an increase in food production is expected to follow from the application of existing agricultural techniques and technologies to areas where they have not yet been used. In addition, however, improvements in food production are envisaged from the results of research and development of various kinds:

1. It has been noted that one of the problems of the 'wet tropics' is the lack of nutritious foods. Very little research has been carried out aimed at the improvement of the nutritional quality of tropical foods or the introduction of new food types into the tropics.
2. The difficulties of the Green Revolution — whose crops were developed to make highest use of fertilizers and irrigation and therefore need careful attention — are seen to be countered by the development of new tough strains or the improvement of existing hardy grain crops. The intention now is to find or develop crops which will survive and prosper under extremely severe and erratic climatic conditions. Millet and sorghum are examples of existing hardy crops. By comparison with farming in the temperate climates, very little research and development has been carried out to improve tropical agriculture (except in relation to cash crops such as tea and coffee).
3. The management of wild herds. For example on the African grasslands, eland — a type of buck — are resistant to the diseases which affect cattle, do not denude the vegetation and are more drought resistant than cattle.
4. Ocean farming and the water culture of fish.
5. The production of synthetic foods from oil waste by the growing of selected strains of micro-organisms. These micro-organisms are then a protein-rich food. Rank-Hovis-MacDougall and BP already have experimental schemes.
6. Finally, to state the obvious: in farming, climate is one of the most significant factors of all. Many schemes have been suggested related to the modification of climate on a mass scale. On a less futuristic level Pirie has written

   Changing the weather is not, however, the only direction of progress. Unpredictability causes serious losses because, through fear of worsening weather, crops may be harvested before they reach their full yield, or they may be damaged by an unexpected deterioration. The US President's Science Advisory Committee estimates that a world wide, completely accurate, forecast of the weather two weeks in advance would increase yields by 5 per cent. That would be worth more than £1000 million a year. We may wonder why meteorological research is not more adequately endowed.

Taken all in all the optimistic forecasts of potential food resources vary from Pirie, who states:

At many points there is great scope for further research, but the vigorous application of existing knowledge on a world wide scale could increase immensely the amount of food produced. The extent of the possible increase is a matter of opinion. But only a very cautious prophet would predict less than doubling . . .

to those who envisage the feasibility of feeding 60 billion.

Whereas the pessimistic outlook varies with the combination and permutation of the negative aspects of the above arguments, the FAO seems doubtful about the ability of the developing world to keep pace with its estimates of the need for a 75% increase in food production over the period 1965–80 and an increase of 225% over the period 1965–2000. The authors of *The Limits to Growth* predict a 'collapse' due to food shortage before the year 2100, whereas the *Blueprint for Survival* predicts collapse and advocates the creation of a new social system based upon decentralization and self-sufficiency. While feeling great personal sympathy for many of the communitarian ideals present in scenarios such as those prepared by the *Blueprint*, the author has to agree with Richard Neuhaus. In his book *In Defence of the People* Neuhaus has written 'the delight of achieving an organically pure eco-diet is frivolous in a world where twelve thousand brothers and sisters die from starvation each day'. The danger in self-sufficiency is the short step to isolationism. In an attempt to counter such a tendency, while maintaining the benefits of self-reliance, certain international networks are currently fostering programs of self-sufficient development (endogenous development). These programs stress the role of appropriate technologies. It remains to be seen whether these projects can make a significant contribution. The affluent rich can afford to take the life of a 'gentleman farmer' as a serious objective — but the third world needs to eat.

The common factor between most, pessimists or optimists, is their tendency to view the situation in aggregation — present famines are seen as forerunners of world famine; present success in high yield or irrigation is seen as the harbinger of huge harvests on a world-wide scale.

Malnutrition results from poverty — not inadequate supplies of food

We have just considered the implications for future food resources of the debate about increasing the quantities of food grown. At the end of their analysis of the agricultural sub-system of the MIT model — which treated the problem of food as a question of aggregated world production — Marstrand and Pavitt concluded:

> Our own opinion is that, although there must clearly be limits to the world's capacity to produce food, the combination of technical progress and the rational use of the world's food-producing resources could put off these physical limits well beyond the time horizon of the World 3 model. However, we see the major problem of feeding the world elsewhere, in politics rather than in physical limits. [World 3 model = model used in *The Limits to Growth*].

McLean and Hopkins have characterized such an approach to the problem of food production as 'the distribution approach'. By 'distribution' they refer to the irregularities which exist within and between nations. One of the basic conclusions of this approach is that the world is capable of feeding its present and future population (using the methods outlined above), but that the barriers to such a rational solution lie at an international level in the regional distribution of power and at a local and national level in the irregularities of wealth in the social system. We now turn to an elaboration of some of the arguments which lead to, support and derive from such a conclusion.

1. NUTRITIONAL STANDARDS

In 1972 Professor Georg Borgstrom, leading international authority on food utilization and world nutrition, stated 'The phenomenon of world nutrition is, however, to a major degree due to a shortage of protein'. Ever since the Second World War nutrition experts have concentrated upon the supposition that the total supply of the world's protein is insufficient to meet world protein needs. And as such the solution advocated has been to feed 'more protein to those who are suffering from protein deficiency'.

By contrast Professor Leonard Joy has summarized the results of recent research into the nature of protein deficiency as follows:

> Paradoxically enough, most of those suffering from protein deficiency eat more than enough protein to meet their protein requirements. However, because they do not eat, in total, enough

calories, the protein that they eat is not utilized as protein for growth or maintenance of body tissue but as calories to supply their energy needs. People whose calorie intakes are adequate are not generally to be found suffering from protein deficiencies.

He then discusses three misconceptions relating to the need for protein in human diet which have exacerbated the understanding of the role of protein in nutrition and the total amount required on a world basis. The first is that there is 'a human requirement for animal protein'. Joy denies this and affirms that, on the contrary, human requirements for protein can be met entirely from vegetable sources, provided that their calorie needs are satisfied and the proteins are properly balanced. There also remains a problem that vitamin B12 is available only in animals and animal products (including milk and eggs) but not in vegetables. The second misconception is that amino-acid fortification is of significant value in repairing inadequacies in protein intake. (Amino-acids are the basic substances necessary for the body to make new proteins and of which all proteins are made). In fact if the person's calorie intake is insufficient his body cannot utilize this additional amino-acid in the way that amino-acids should be used — for tissue building or renewal — the amino-acid will simply be used as calories to supply their energy needs.

The third misconception is the 'statistical fallacy' which is employed in the calculations that leads the UN (FAO/WHO/UNICEF) to talk of a 'protein crisis'. The fallacy is embodied in the following argument. Since there is considerable variability of individual protein requirements, individuals with intakes equal to mean requirements stand a chance of having less than their needs; consequently, *recommended* levels of intake for individuals should, for safety's sake, be above *mean requirement* levels. From this it is wrongly argued that target national supplies would, with ideal distribution, need to be the sum of individuals' *recommended* intakes (i.e. mean requirements plus 20% . . .). If this should sound an expensive national insurance premium, consider the next stage of the argument which says that, since the distribution of intakes has a far greater range than the distribution of needs, then national targets have to be raised by the amount which ensures that everybody's requirements will be met. The calculation to determine how much this should be is made assuming that the skewness of distribution remains constant (i.e. that everybody's intake is increased by the same amount). It has been calculated that the application of this logic to Maharashtra would require a *target for protein supplies of almost four times the sum of individual mean requirements.* Such a target would be grossly unrealistic, totally unnecessary and, if taken seriously, dangerously counterproductive. It has therefore been rightly concluded that effort should be directed to 'those dwelling in the lower part of the consumption distribution'.

Joy has concluded that the UN identification of a 'protein crisis' based on such a misconception not only grossly exaggerates the protein problem but it leads to proposals for dangerously unrealistic targets. In addition these targets are expensive not only through their exaggeration but in the type of food they advocate: fish, milk and meat. 'Neither poor people nor poor governments can afford to meet protein-calorie requirements in such ways and the attempt to do so could mean a gross misallocation of resources'.

The extent to which the FAO itself has recognized that its previous standards were too high may be seen by the variation between the 1950 and 1973 'recommended "safe" levels of protein intake' (gm/kg body weight/day):

	Adult	18 month child
1950	2½	3½
1973	½	1½

At the same time FAO has recently estimated that the average calories needed are 2354 and that 2420 are available at the market level. As one critic has summarized this new knowledge:

> The *per capita* availability of food grains is about 2½ times the requirement. If protein (all sources) is taken as the main qualitative measure factor and its daily requirement at 70 grams *per capita*, the total availability is also more than twice the requirement.

But the international bodies have yet to realize the implications of these reassessments of nutritional requirements, nutrient content of vegetable foods and aggregate availability of food. As McLean and Hopkins put it:

> From the twin premises that there is enough food in the world and that the nutrient composition of much food is also satisfactory, nutritionists have been forced to the conclusion that the nature of the 'food problem' is one of distribution.

The problem of 'distribution' is not the malfunctioning of the channels by which AID program food is distributed to the needy. Within nations it is the inequitable distribution of income whereby those without incomes are unable to buy the sufficiency of food that exists on the world market. As Joy has concluded:

> The basic fact about the nutrition problem is that it is primarily a poverty problem: a problem of ineffective demand rather than of ineffective supply; for food not just for protein.

2. INEQUALITIES

Such an identification of the 'food problem' is further substantiated by an understanding of other inequalities in relation to food production which exist between countries — most of which contribute to the inequalities within individual nations themselves.

(a) *Cash crops:* Hundreds of millions in the tropics are forced to shrink their food production in order to raise peanuts, cotton, sugar, bananas, coffee, tea, cocoa, for export in order that the nations, multinational firms and individual landowners, can accrue foreign currency. The third world supplies total world needs for these commodities. It is also a major supplier of oils and fats to the industrialized nations.

(b) *Protein:* Ehrlich has written that 'poor countries are major net exporters of protein'. Indeed the USA ranks next to the UK as the largest importer of protein and the USA is the largest importer of fish protein. Much of this comes from off the coast of Peru — caught by the Peruvian fishing fleet. Borgstrom has written:

> The Peruvian catches alone would suffice to raise nutritional standards with respect to protein for the undernourished on the entire South American continent to Southern European level. The amount of protein extracted (1966—68) exceeds by one half the meat protein produced in South America (including Argentina) and is three times the milk protein raised.

The cruel irony is that this protein is generally used to feed the animals of the developed nations. Borgstrom considers this protein export a 'treacherous exchange'.

(c) '9/10 of the exports of poor countries consist of food, feed and agricultural products': summarizes (a) and (b).

3. SOCIAL RESTRUCTURING

At the local level the identification of the food problem as one of poverty has been further substantiated by the realization that Engels reached a century ago: 'The labour power to be employed on this area increases together with the population'. Although population is increasing, so are the numbers who could till the land. Yet in the developing countries masses of people are unable to find work while machines only lie idle (and rust) when they need repair.

The basic conclusion from the above is that policies to end food shortages should 'seek to generate incomes among the poor'. The reassessment of nutritional standards, the relative failure of the Green Revolution and the acknowledgement of the progress made in European farming productivity in the early 19th century with relatively simple improvements in tools and methods, all point to the encouragement of hardy crops such as millet and the introduction of the relatively simple techniques as means to follow at the same time as policies directed towards the reduction of poverty.

Another conclusion has been that with the new understanding of the food problem an alternative objective, which would achieve the same results, would be the restructuring of the social system as has taken place in China and Cuba where starvation has been eliminated.

Hopkins and MacLean concluded, in relation to Leonard Joy's proposition, 'It should of course be realized that the timescale for such superstructural changes is similar to that required for the alteration of political realities'. And the insights gained from the analysis can be as sombre as those of the pessimists in relation to food supply if the forecasters see the political situation as intransigent. On the other hand, those forecasters who see the possibility of instituting changes of policy can make very hopeful forecasts, especially when the possibilities for political change are combined with the opportunities for increased productivity which were discussed above under 'methods of increasing productivity'. Either way the introduction of the political perspective shows the extreme limitations of concentrating solely upon the physical limits of food production.

Reading

ESSENTIAL

3.1   Meadows *et al.* (1972) (*ref. 1.1*), Chapter 2 'The Limits to Exponential Growth', especially pp. 45—54.
3.2   Marstrand, P. and Pavitt, K., 'The Agricultural Subsystem', Chapter 5 in Cole *et al.* (1973) (*ref. 1.3*), pp. 56—65.
3.3   Pirie, N. W., *Food Resources Conventional and Novel*. Penguin, 1969, Chapter 2 'Capabilities of Conventional Agriculture'.
3.4   George, Susan, *How the Other Half Dies*, the real reasons for world hunger. Penguin, 1976.
3.5   Marstrand, P. and Rush, H., 'Food & Agriculture: when food is not enough — the World Food Paradox', Chapter 4 in Freeman and Jahoda (eds.) (1978) (*ref. 1.8*) pp. 79—112.

ADDITIONAL

3.6   Bahr, H. M., Chadwick, B. A. and Thomas, D. L. (eds.), *Population, Resources and the Future — non-Malthusian perspectives.* Brigham Young UP, 1974.

3.7   Beckermann, Wilfred, *In Defence of Economic Growth.* Jonathan Cape, 1974, pp. 235–240.
      Food and Population

3.8   Borgstrom, Georg, *The Hungry Planet.* Macmillan, 1965.
      The modern world at the edge of famine; protein shortage discussed in detail.

3.9   Borgstrom, Georg, *Too Many.* Macmillan, 1969.
      Very similar to previous reference.

3.10 Buringh, P., van Heemst, H. D. J. and Staring, G. J., *Computation of the Absolute Maximum Food Production of the World.* Wageningen: Agricultural University, 1975.

3.11 Dawson, O. L., *Communist China's Agriculture: its Development and Future Potential.* NY Praeger, 1970.

3.12 DeTwyler, Thomas R., *Man's Impact on Environment.* McGraw Hill, 1971.
      Limitations of monoculture: Part 7.

3.13 Dunman, J., *Agriculture: Capitalist and Socialist.* London: Lawrence & Wishart, 1975.

3.14 Eberstadt, N., 'Myths of the World Food Crisis', *New York Review of Books,* **23**, (2), Feb. 1976, pp. 32–37.

3.15 Edwards, Angela and Rogers, Alan (ed.), *Agricultural Resources.* Faber and Faber, 1974.
      An introduction to the farming industry of the UK.

3.16 Ehrlich (1970) (*ref. 2.13*).
      Pessimistic outlook for food production, Chapters 4 and 5.

3.17 The Ecologist (1972) (*ref. 1.5*), Appendix C, pp. 117–128.
      Pessimistic.

3.18 Food and Agriculture Organisation (FAO), *Provisional Indicative Plan for Agricultural Development Vol I, II, III.* FAO, 1969.
      An overview.
      The FAO also bring out yearly reports on 'The State of Food and Agriculture', 'Statistics' and 'Problem Identification'.

3.19 Frankel, F. R., *India's Green Revolution: Economic Gains and Political Costs.* Princeton University Press, 1971.

3.20 Farvar, Taghi M. and Milton, John P., *The Careless Technology.* Stacey, 1973.
      Chapters on the limitations of monoculture and large scale irrigation. Generally sceptical about technology as it has so far been applied to development.

3.21 GB Select Cttee on Overseas Development Session 1975–76, *The World Food Crisis & Third World Development: Implications for UK Policy.* London: HMSO, 1976.

3.22 Hayami, Y. and Ruttan, V., *Agricultural Development.* John Hopkins Press, 1971.

3.23 Johnson, Gale, *World Agriculture in Disarray.* Macmillan, 1973. Refers to the need for industrialized countries to reform policies which are protecting farmers in those countries from world prices and are thus leading to higher food costs in the industrialized countries.

3.24 Johnson, D. G., *World Food Problems and Prospects.* Washington DC: American Enterprise Institute of Public Policy Research, 1975.

3.25 Joy, Leonard, 'Food and Nutrition Planning', *IDS reprint No. 107.* Sussex, 1973.

3.26 King, M. H., *et al.* (eds.), *Nutrition for developing countries.* OUP, 1972.

3.27 Lerza, C. and Jacobson, M., *Food for People Not for Profit.* Ballantine, 1975.

3.28 Lipton, M., *Why Poor People Stay Poor.* London: Temple Smith, 1977.

3.29 Maddox, John, *The Doomsday Syndrome.* Macmillan, 1972. Chapter 3: The End of the Lode. Optimistic and ever dismissive of *Limits*-type arguments.

3.30 Mellanby, K., *Can Britain Feed Itself?* London: Merlin Press, 1975.

3.31 McLean, Mick and Hopkins, Mike, 'Problems of World Food and Agriculture: Projections, models and possible approaches', *Futures.* August 1974, pp. 309—318.

3.32 Lappé, Francis Moore and Collins, Joseph, *Food First: Beyond the Myth of Scarcity.* Boston: Houghton Mifflin Co, 1977.

3.33 Organization for Economic Cooperation and Development, *Agricultural Projections for 1975 and 1985.* Europe, North America, Japan, Oceania. OECD, 1968. Data on the production and consumption of major foodstuffs.

3.34 Paddock, William and Paul, *Famine 1975.* Little, Brown, 1967. 'America's decision: who will survive?' is the sub-title.

3.35 Pimentel, D., *et al.,* 'Food Production and the Energy Crisis', *Science,* (1973), **182**, pp. 443—449. Discusses the efficiency of agriculture with respect to energy.

3.36 Poleman, Thomas T. and Freebaum, Donald K., *Food, Population and Employment.* Prager Publishers, 1973.

3.37 UN Department of Economic and Social Affairs (1973) (*ref. 2.21*), Chapter XII: Population and Food. An excellent survey of the field.

3.38 Wilson, Angus, *As if by Magic.* Penguin, 1976. The Green Revolution seen through the eyes of a novelist.

3.39 'Science and food for man', *Impact of Science on Society,* **XXIV**, (2), Apr.—June 1974 (special issue).

3.40 'The hungry planet', (a series of articles), *New Scientist,* 7 Nov. 1974, pp. 388–44.
3.41 'Running out of food', *Newsweek,* 11 Nov. 1974, pp. 12–20. A special report on the world food crisis.
3.42 'Boost for credit rating of organic farmers', *Science,* **189,** 1975, pp. 777. Organic farmers were three times more efficient in energy terms.
3.43 *Science and Public Policy,* **3,** (3), June 1976. Several articles on food in developing countries.
3.44 *Ambio,* **6,** (2–3), 1977, pp. 137–140. Whole issue on nitrogen.
3.45 'The global political economy of food', *International Organization,* **32,** (3) (Summer 1978), special issue.
3.46 Abelson, P. H. (ed.), *Food: Politics Economics Nutrition and Research.* Amer. Assoc. for Adv of Science, 1975.
3.47 Austin, J. E., *Agribusiness in Latin America.* Praeger, 1974.
3.48 Bardhan, K. and P., 'The green revolution and socio-economic tensions: the case of India', *Int. Social Science Journal,* **XXV,** (3), 1973, pp. 285–92.
3.49 Feder, E., 'How agribusiness operates in underdeveloped agricultures', *Development and Change,* **7,** Oct. 1976.
3.50 Kropotkin, P., *Fields Factories and Workshops Tomorrow.* Ed. by Colin Ward. Allen and Unwin, 1974.
3.51 Lappé, F. M. and Collins, J., 'More food means more hunger', *Futurist,* **XI,** (2), Apr. 1977, pp. 90–93.
3.52 Merrill, R. (ed.), *Radical Agriculture.* Harper and Row, 1976.
3.53 Reutlinger, S., 'Food insecurity: magnitude and remedies', *World Development,* **6,** (6), June 1978, pp. 797–811.
3.54 Schumacher, E. F., *Small is Beautiful,* a study of economics as if people mattered. Blond and Briggs, 1973.

JOURNALS DIRECTLY RELEVANT TO FOOD

Ceres.
Development Forum (UN Geneva).
Food Policy (Guildford).

Points for discussion or essays

1. Discuss the assumptions and evidence adopted by the various schools of thought on the existence, extent and causes of the present world-wide starvation. In this respect how does the present compare with past eras? (*refs. 3.6, 3.7, 3.8, 3.25, 3.31, 3.37*).

2. Malthus said: 25 years doubling time for population — food cannot keep pace. Was he right? If not why not? If so, what happened? (*ref. 3.2*).
3. Discuss the criteria of nutrition. (*refs. 3.8, 3.9, 3.16, 3.25, 3.31*).
4. Discuss methods of increasing production
   (a) in industrialized countries
   (b) in developing countries
   (*refs. 3.2, 3.3, 3.22, 3.29, 3.50, 3.52, 3.54*).
5. What is The Green Revolution? What is its role in food production programs? Assess its contribution to these programs. (*refs. 3.19, 3.36, 3.38*).
6. Discuss the protein vs. calorie debate and its implications for forecasts of food resources. (*ref. 3.25*).
7. What is the relation between agricultural production and population? (*ref. 3.37*). What are the social attitudes of those who have written about the relationship between population and agriculture?
8. '. . . half the world's people are conveniently forgotten by the food companies'.

   > How often we see in developing countries that the poorer the economic outlook, the more important the small luxury of a flavored soft drink or smoke . . . to the dismay of many would-be benefactors, the poorer the malnourished are, the more likely they are to spend a disproportionate amount of whatever they have on some luxury rather than on what they need . . . Observe, study, learn [how to sell in rapidly changing rural societies]. We try to do it at IFF. It seems to pay off for us. Perhaps it will for you too.
   > Board Chairman,
   > International Flavors and Fragrances (IFF)

   Discuss the role of large food companies in relation to both industrialized and developing countries. (*refs. 3.4, 3.27, 3.32, 3.47*).
9. Discuss the relationship between food production and energy. (*refs. 3.35, 3.52*).

Questions related to *The Limits to Growth*

1. Discuss the assumptions, evidence and conclusions of the *Limits to Growth* team. Do you agree or disagree with their views? Justify your position.

2. Of the many assumptions made by the *Limits to Growth* team, Marstrand and Pavitt consider two as critical:
   (a) as people get richer, they spend a diminishing percentage of wealth on food;
   (b) each increase in the production of food will require a greater increment of investment i.e. there are diminishing returns to agricultural investment.

   Marstrand and Pavitt state that the first assumption has been confirmed through observation, but the second has not been confirmed by historical experience. Elaborate their arguments supporting this statement and consider its effect upon the conclusions reached by the *Limits* team. (*ref. 3.2*).

3. In the model diminishing returns to agricultural investment becomes a serious problem when the world's population reaches about 20,000 million (5 x present population). According to Marstrand and Pavitt this depends critically upon the validity of the assumptions made in the model about the costs of developing arable land and about future trends in land yield. Discuss the effect of these assumptions upon the results of the model. (*ref. 3.2*).

4. The authors of *The Limits to Growth* state: 'the primary resource for producing food is land'. But it is only one? Discuss the relative merits of this emphasis upon land (*ref. 2.3*).

Chapter Four
Non-renewable Resources
(and Postscript on Energy)

The Natural Resources Committee created by the National Academy of Sciences in response to a request from President Kennedy in 1961 defined a natural resource as 'any naturally occurring element, product, or force that can be utilized by man in his contemporary environment'. Such a definition of resources has been seen as characteristic of man's egoism, of man's dominion in relation to his environment: there to be used as the interests of man dictate. Such a view of resources contrasts with a more reciprocal image of man as an element of nature, as a part of the whole, as living in harmony with his environment. The debate on this subject is wide ranging. Here we are mainly concerned with the future availability of non-renewable natural resources for consumption by man: metals, industrial materials (asbestos etc.), construction materials (cement etc.), and excluding materials that are grown (e.g. timber).

The authors of *The Limits to Growth* state 'Given present consumption rates and the projected increase in these rates, the great majority of the currently important non-renewable resources will be extremely costly in 100 years from now', and that 'as long as the driving feedback loops of population and industrial growth continue to generate more people and a higher resource demand per capita, the system is being pushed towards its limit — the depletion of the earth's non-renewable resources'. The *Blueprint for Survival* stated 'Present reserves of all but a few metals will be exhausted within 50 years, if consumption rates continue to grow as they are'. An Australian philosopher, John Passmore has written equally confidently, but without specifying a time limit: 'We can be certain that some day our society will run out of resources but we do not know when it will do so or what resources it will continue to demand'.

Yet Norman McRae, writing in the *Economist*, happily informs us that with the aid of the new sensors, carried by satellites, which are now available to geologists, vastly increased reserves of fossil fuels and minerals will soon be available for man's use. 'My own guess', he writes of fossil fuels in particular, 'is that we will have an embarrassingly large fuel surplus . . . by the year 2012'. The nuclear physicist Alvin Weinberg is no less confident that 'the problem of resource depletion is a phony'. With the exception of phosphorus, he tells us, 'the most essential resources are virtually inexhaustible'. The physical chemist Eugene Rabinowitch, editor of the influential and respected *Bulletin of the Atomic Scientists*, is equally reassuring. Modern science, he informs his readers, is 'showing us ways to create wealth from widely available raw materials — common minerals, air, sea water —

with the aid of potentially unlimited sources of energy (fusion power, solar energy)'. If these scientists and economists are right, then there is simply no 'problem of resource depletion'. But they stand in diametric opposition to the scientists and economists mentioned earlier. Both positions — imminent depletion of resources and the imminent availability of inexhaustible wealth — are held by experts; highly qualified and respected men. Whom are we to believe?

Many writers, including the authors of *The Limits to Growth*, have only considered the physical factors affecting the availability of non-renewable resources. In this respect, some have considered the outlook to be bleak (*Limits*), in opposition to those who do not see pressing physical limits to resources availability. Other writers, who might be either optimistic or pessimistic vis-a-vis physical limits, have argued that consideration of physical factors, to the exclusion of socio-economic and political factors, is extremely limited. We will first outline the arguments of the optimists and pessimists in relation to the physical nature of resources. Following this we will give some of the socio-economic and political perspectives.

The optimists

With differing degrees of emphasis their case rests upon two main pillars:

1. PHYSICAL AVAILABILITY OF RESOURCES

'A large portion of the earth's land mass has hardly been looked at in detail . . .' Large deposits of almost all the metals have been discovered recently. The regularity with which these discoveries have been made has led to expectations that those discoveries will be augmented by others. Exploration and production using existing tried and tested methods are therefore expected to continue. There are also novel but relatively easily accessible resources. There are an estimated 10^{12} tons of manganese nodules in the Pacific Ocean; these nodules contain around 0.25 to 0.30% cobalt, 0.20 to 0.75% copper, 0.42 to 1% nickel and 16 to 25% manganese. The massive ocean dredgers needed for this type of exploitations have already been built for, amongst others, a company once owned by the late Howard Hughes. It is anticipated that there are vast quantities of iron, aluminium and zinc on or just beneath the ocean floor.

Beyond these relatively simple extensions of present day resources lie others of varying degrees of accessibility. Air, water and earth (excluding rock) contain, between them, traces of almost every known substance. One cubic mile of sea water contains around 47 tons each of aluminium, iron and zinc and there are about 330—350 million cubic miles of sea water. The earth's crust is 25 to 40 miles thick: given the natural concentrations of the key metals in the earth's crust, as indicated by a large number of random samples, the total natural occurrence of most metals in only the top mile of the earth's crust has been estimated to be about a million times as great as present known reserves. Far below the crust itself lies the iron-nickel core which contains an estimated 10^{20} metric tons of nickel-iron which could last, at present consumption rates, for about 10^{11} years. Finally the extension of present embryonic interplanetary exploration will enable recovery of easily locatable and easily extractable deposits from other planets. The last two (the core and the planets) are not immediately exploitable, but they have been proposed as future possibilities.

2. TECHNICAL PROGRESS

'The main escape hatch from scarcity is technological advance across a broad front . . .' The broad front includes exploration, mining and processing the raw material, creation of synthetic materials, finding new uses for old materials or substituting alternatives and, the recycling and the more efficient use of materials.

The new methods of exploration made possible by satellites and new electronic detecting devices have only just begun to be used. The advances made by science and technology in the mining field have led on the one hand to the exploitation of fields previously considered too low grade to be worth mining — in the 1880s the lowest grade of copper ore which could economically be handled was 3%; it is now 0.4%. On the other hand these advances have led to the reprocessing of waste materials from previously mined substances such as the old waste dumps on the South African gold fields. These types of technical advance have made the extraction of minerals from earth and sea water a possibility. Further the large scale exploitation of solar energy and power from nuclear energy are seen as the means by which these operations will be carried out. Besides which there is also great scope for reducing the energy used per unit of output.

Technical advances over the past hundred years have by and large kept pace with demand (real costs have remained roughly constant); some say that the technical advances have in fact created that demand. Either way this progress is not seen as coming to a sudden halt.

The combination of vast resources and continual technical progress lead to different estimates of the numbers of people who could live at current American standards of material living, varying from 7 to 1000 times the present world population.

The pessimists

The pessimists counter each of the above assertions. In relation to the extent of resources three major arguments are employed. Firstly the fact is stressed that the earth does not contain limitless quantities of anything. It is a finite body. Here frequent mention is made of the similarity between the earth and a spaceship and that the earth forms a 'closed system':

> If there is an infinite system, then there are an infinite number of resources to be exploited. You can be just as careless and stupid as you want, since there are an infinite number of resources out there and we'll never run out. And there's an infinite amount of space in which you can get rid of all your filth as you waste those resources. But in a closed system you can't do that — and that's the kind of system we're in. We have anything but an infinite number of resources.

This is emphasized by Ehrlich 'It is important to demonstrate that we are for practical purposes limited to our own small planet'.

Given this, together with the present growth rates of consumption, the projected sizes of population are so great that it will be impossible to meet future resource requirements. It is also assumed that the future consumption of resources will follow the present pattern set by the USA. As Meadows put it, 'We assume that, as the rest of the world develops economically, it will follow basically the US pattern of consumption'. Estimates of total US utilization of raw materials currently range from 30 to 50% of world production, with a projection of current trends for 1980 between 50 and 80%. Even when one considers that the US has less than 6% of the world population, those figures do not accurately describe the extent to which US consumption is ahead of the rest. The US industrial system consumes enormous quantities of materials. Should developing countries want to reach American standards of living, and use her mode of using materials, the consequences are even clearer:

> To raise all the 3.6 billion people of the world of 1970 to the American standard of living would require the extraction of almost 30 billion tons of iron, more than 500 million tons of copper and lead, more than 300 million tons of zinc, about 50 million tons of tin, as well as enormous quantities of other minerals. That means the extraction of some 75 times as much iron as is now extracted annually, 100 times as much copper, 200 times as much lead, 75 times as much zinc and 250 times as much tin . . . Of course, to raise the standard of living of the projected world population of the year 2000 to today's American standard would require doubling all of the above figures.

Thirdly, it is claimed that all the easily obtainable minerals, in the sense of location, have already been located and assessed. To exploit others is both economically too costly and technically improbable.

In relation to the role to be played by technical progress, the pessimists are as adamant as on the extent of resources. The belief in the use of science and technology to find methods of extracting smaller and smaller quantities of a mineral from its parent rock is not one which can be relied upon. The technical difficulties are enormous. No one can predict that a certain advance will definitely be made, so not much hope is held out for 'meeting the scarcity problem by such exotic technologies as deep sea mining of extractive minerals'.

Essentially the same argument applies to the use of science and technology in finding substitutes for materials which are rapidly becoming exhausted. Professor Mishan has written:

> And though in the constructs of economists there are always substitute resources waiting to be used whenever the price of an existing resource begins to rise, there is no knowing yet what, if anything, will substitute for a range of such apparently essential metals — lead, mercury, zinc, silver, gold, platinum, copper, tungsten — that will become increasingly scarce before the end of the century.

A Professor of Geology at Stanford University has reinforced the economists' position by writing that

> nothing now known can take the place of steel where strength is needed, as in great skyscrapers and cans or in the high temperature alloys for parts of a jet engine, nothing now known will substitute for cobalt in the manufacture of the strong permanent magnets needed in all modern communications systems and no other metal will, like mercury, become liquid at ordinary temperatures and therefore be usable in temperature and pressure control equipment.

The limitations of technical progress are seen to be most obvious in the case of the much vaunted production of unlimited nuclear energy by fusion. It is pointed out that nuclear fusion was predicted for 1975 but that several of the requisite technological breakthroughs have not occurred in time to make that date a reality. While significant advances were reported in 1978, technical progress is not the only stumbling block. Besides its high cost Ehrlich considers it unlikely that cheap nuclear energy could greatly reduce the cost of mining, because most mining would still continue to be subterranean as there are definite limits to the feasible depth of open cast mining. As he points out vis-a-vis the general application of nuclear energy: nuclear plants produce only electrical energy; and electrical energy constituted only 19 per cent of the total energy consumed in the US in 1960:

> The reality is that even the achievement of a breeder reactor offers no guarantee of unlimited mineral resources in the face of geological limitations and expanding populations with increased per-capita demands, even over the middle term. To assume such for the long term would be sheer folly.

The general conclusion is that 'average rock will never be mined'.

Even in cases where some technical progress is foreseen it is no panacea:

> Obviously, there will be new discoveries and advances in mining technology, but these are likely to provide us with only a limited stay of execution.

But the pessimists have a second line of criticism beyond lack of resources and uncertainty of technical innovation. Even if the resources were discovered, and technical progress made their exploitation possible then at present rates of growth of resource consumption there would be three unwelcome consequences. The amounts of energy required firstly to convert the raw materials into usable resources and then the resources into goods, would produce too much heat for the eco-system of the earth (this will be further explored in the chapter on pollution). The costs of using such great quantities of energy would be prohibitive. The amounts of waste produced in isolating the materials from their parent rock would be disruptive to the environment immediately adjacent to the mining operations. 'The enormous quantities of unusable waste produced for each ton of metal are more easily disposed of on a blue-print than in the field'.

In brief we see that the optimists foresee the availability of vast reserves of resources and the possibility of technical developments necessary to make them available to man, whereas the pessimists deny both.

While most writers on the subject of resources can be placed in one or other camp, there is a smaller group who have distinctive arguments to add to the debate. Whether they support either the optimistic or the pessimistic prognosis they do so in such a way that takes note of socio-economic and political factors.

Socio-economic and political perspectives

These stem from a historical consideration of resource availability, and the economic aspect of technology in resource exploitation. They give rise to a definition of 'resources' which changes with time and social development.

In 1865 Stanley Jevons, a noted English economist, published a short book called *The Coal Question*, in which he anticipated a dwindling supply of coal and, therefore, a definite upper limit upon the capacity of the steel industry (and hence the economy as a whole) to experience further growth. Several things happened to disprove his forecast: large reserves of coal were found; the coking process was discovered; other energy sources were discovered (e.g. oil) and greater economy in energy use was developed.

In the 1890s W. J. McGee and Gifford Pinchot warned the United States about the imminent depletion of oil, coal and minerals within a matter of decades and urged upon the nation rigorous policies of resource conservation. In 1908 President Theodore Roosevelt was alarmed at the low levels, and impending exhaustion, of mineral reserves in the USA. He called for a survey of resources which located more resources. Similar surveys in response to similar alarms have often been conducted since. A 1929 study concluded 'it is clear that the world's resources [of] lead cannot meet present demand' and 'the known reserves of tin . . . do not seem to satisfy the ever increasing demand of the industrial nations for more than 10 years'. After the Second World War the Paley Report was prepared in response to a fear in the USA concerning increasing scarcity of domestic mineral supplies. Another study, carried out in 1944, gave estimates of available reserves which, had they been correct, would have meant that by 1973 half the products on the list would already have been exhausted. In particular, the USA would have already run out of tin, nickel, zinc, lead and manganese. In the face of these forecasts more deposits of these minerals have been found in the USA during the 1950s than during the previous twenty-five years.

This continual confounding of prophecy aids and abets the belief in the possibility of further abundancy and it gives the lie to present forecasts of imminent exhaustion. But more importantly in the present context, it raises the question as to why, however fast demand expanded and for however long, new mineral reserves were found?

A World Bank report answered:

> The reason why we do not know the absolute limits of resources we have is simple and does not even require recourse to elaborate arguments about the wonders of technology. We do not know because no one has as yet found it necessary to know and therefore gone about taking an accurate inventory.

Estimates of reserves at any one time never represent true reserves in the sense of being all that can be found, irrespective of the demand and the price. They are only 'conservative contingency forecasts by the exploration companies and they are related to a certain price: if the price is higher, more resources can be exploited commercially'.

For example, known iron ore reserves would apparently be doubled at a price 30 to 40% higher than the current price. And the reserve estimates for copper, which are now about 3.5 times higher than in 1935, would be expected to rise eightfold if the price were to rise threefold. The same report continues, 'the authors of *The Limits to Growth* allow for the effects of higher prices on exploration for new reserves by the 'generous' assumption that reserves could increase by 5 times over the next 100 years, but what appears to be an act of generosity turns out to be an unduly conservative assumption in the light of historical evidence and recent finds'.

Similarly technological developments are seen as taking place in response to demand and therefore the onus for development does not lie within technology itself but within the society that uses the technology.

Not only does the quantity of a resource and the quality of its related technology change with time, the very nature of what is defined as a 'resource' can and does change:

> A hundred years ago oil, natural gas and uranium would not have featured in an inventory of world energy resources. At that point in time the inventory would have consisted of easily accessible coal, peat, wood, animal power and other forms of energy used in traditional societies. A hundred years hence the inventory will doubtless be different from one attempted now and might include thorium and solar energy for example.

Arguments such as these led Freeman, in the *Critique of Limits to Growth*, to conclude that 'the concept of "reserves" in most resource forecasting is techno-economic rather than geo-physical and the world reserves of most known materials would probably have been under-estimated by orders of magnitude'. Later in the same book Page states, 'The most pressing limits to growth in resource usage are not geological. . . . The critical limits for examination therefore, are not so much technological but more economic and social'.

Such a perspective on the nature of resources takes particular exception to the *Limits to Growth* assumption that 'as the rest of the world develops economically, it will follow basically the US pattern of consumption'. (The degree to which the US differs from the rest of the world in resource consumption has been mentioned above and need not be repeated here). If resource use is socially determined and if the US is so different from the rest of the world, is it reasonable to assume that developing countries will follow suit? Several arguments are used to challenge such an assumption.

For the past two decades one of the guiding lights in the United

Nations Development Programme has been the belief that rapid industrialization is the means of improving the standard of living of the people. Therefore much time and effort has been put into encouraging such development. Between 1957 and 1967, India increased its steel consumption by 41%, against only 12% in the USA; yet in actual consumption figures, the US increased from 568 to 634 kilos per capita, India from 9.2 to 13 kilos per capita. The quantities involved neither show an overnight switch to American patterns nor do they justify the scaremongering involved in stating that the developing countries, by following the US standards, will rapidly absorb vast quantities of materials.

A second argument refers to the different life styles throughout the world. Particular reference is made to China. In terms of GNP it is amongst the lowest in the world alongside India and Pakistan. It cannot be proved that China's ultimate material objectives are not on a par with the USA. Yet reputable foreign observers assure us that poverty, starvation and housing shortages have been eliminated without recourse to a massive increase in GNP. Certain social objectives have therefore been met by means which have not yet entailed any vast consumption of resources.

This fundamental objection to the *Limits to Growth* statement that economic well-being (in the broadest sense of the word) necessarily entails following in the footsteps of the US leads to a conclusion which we have seen in previous chapters: the dangers of aggregation which are present in the *Limits* approach.

The socio-economic and political perspective sees far more dangers in the escalation of the gap in welfare between the rich countries and the poor countries, than in the physical limits of economic growth. The effects of the latter analysis are derived from a *Limits*-type approach which aggregates average 'world' consumption rates and average 'world' population rates.

A good illustration of how social and political events can influence the availability of minerals (and give rise to concern about the future to many people) was the action by the oil exporting countries (OPEC – the Organization of Petroleum Exporting Countries) in October 1973. The OPEC members agreed to reduce the quantities of oil they supplied to the Western Countries, and world oil prices increased three-fold over a couple of months. As a result, the income of the oil exporters increased by several billion dollars, giving them considerably greater power than they have ever had in recent times. The concern being expressed in many quarters is how they will use this economic power; will it be to the good or bad of the world future? This often means will it be to the good of the rich western countries or not?

Since October 1973, the exporters of other minerals have suggested that they might follow the OPEC move. The producers of copper (Chile, Peru, Zambia and Zaire), iron ore (including India and Venezuela), and bauxite (including Jamaica and Guyana), are amongst those who have thought of following OPEC's example. Such activity adds to the concern felt by some people over the stability of the world economy and its long-term prospects.

It should be emphasised that this type of concern is very different from that expressed in *The Limits to Growth*. It derives from political action, not from physical limits. This implies that the solutions are to be found not only through zero growth or small family size, but also through diplomacy and international trade agreements.

Reading

ESSENTIAL

4.1   Page, R. W., 'Non-renewable Resources Sub-system', Chapter 3 in Cole *et al.* (1973), (*ref. 1.3*), pp. 33–42.
4.2   Passmore, John, 'Conservation', Chapter 4 in Passmore (1974), (*ref. 2.4*), pp. 73–100.
4.3   Meadows *et al.* (1972), (*ref. 1.1*), pp. 54–68.
4.4   Page, W. 'Some Non-Fuel Mineral Resources', Chapter 6 in Freeman and Jahoda (eds.) (1978), (*ref. 1.8*), pp. 169–206.

ADDITIONAL

4.5   Beckermann (1974), (*ref. 3.7*), Chapter 8: 'Resources for Growth'.
4.6   Beckmann (1973), (*ref. 2.5*), Chapter 3: 'Resources: Beethoven depleted half of all classical music'.
      Criticises the arguments of *Limits* and other pessimists – their type of thinking could lead to a self-fulfilling prophecy.
4.7   Cloud, Preston, 'Mineral Resources in Fact and Fancy', in H. Daly (ed.), *Toward a Stable State Economy*. W. H. Freeman, 1971.
      A brief summary of the non-renewable resource situation with a commentary on some of the premises of technological optimism.
4.8   Easlea, B., *Liberation and the Aims of Science*. Chatto and Windus, 1973 (also New Jersey: Rowan and Littlefield), esp. Chapters 8, 10, 11, 12.
4.9   The Ecologist (1972), (*ref. 1.5*), Appendix D, Non-renewable Resources.
4.10 Ehrlich (1970), (*ref. 2.13*), pp. 51–63.
4.11 Environmental Studies Board, (National Academy of Science, National Academy of Engineering), *Man, Materials and Environment*. M.I.T. Press, 1973.
      Legislative procedures already exist for coping with pollutant side-effects of resource depletion.

4.12 Falk, A., *This Endangered Planet.* Random House, 1971,
       pp. 139–180.
       A well argued pessimism about limits of resources.
4.13 Friends of the Earth, 'Nearing the Ends of Metal Mining in
       Britain', mimeo, 1972.
       Speaks for itself.
4.14 IBRD (World Bank) Report on the *Limits to Growth.*
       Washington, 1972.
       Challenges *Limits* conclusions.
4.15 Kay, J. A. and Mirrlees, J. A., 'The Desirability of Natural
       Resources Depletion' in D. W. Pearce (ed.), *The Economics
       of Natural Resources Depletion.* Macmillan, 1975.
4.16 Landsberg, Hans H., Fischman, Leonard L. and Fischer, Joseph L.,
       *Resources in America's Future: Patterns of Requirement and
       Availabilities.* John Hopkins Press, 1963.
       'The U.S. historical data do not point to increasing scarcity . . .
       A continued rise in the level of living seems assured', pp. 43–44.
4.17 Leiss, W., *The Domination of Nature.* Braziller, 1972.
4.18 Leiss, William, *The Limits to Satisfaction:* An essay on the
       problem of needs and commodities. Univ. of Toronto, 1976.
       Examines the demand and consumption of resources.
4.19 Maddox, John, (1972), (*ref. 3.29*), Chapter 3, The End of the
       Lode. Refutation of *The Limits to Growth.*
4.20 Maglen, Leo R., 'Non renewable resources and the limits to
       growth: another look', *Search.* Vol 8, No 5, pp. 158–166,
       May 1977.
4.21 Mero, J., 'Oceanic Mineral Resources', *Futures.* December 1969.
       Describes the vast potential resources which exist in the oceans.
4.22 Moran, T., 'The Multinational Corporation versus the Economic
       Nationalist: Independence and Domination in Raw Materials'.
       mimeo.
       Discusses the political implications of resource shortages.
4.23 National Materials Advisory Board (US) *Silver and its applications.*
       US Govt. Printing Office, 1972.
4.24 The *Natural Resources Journal.* 16:4 (Oct. 1976) contains a
       symposium on 'Water Resource management in a changing
       world', pp. 737–974.
4.25 Park, Charles F. Jr., *Affluence in Jeopardy: Minerals and the
       Political Economy.* Freeman, Cooper, 1968.
       Expresses serious doubts regarding possibilities of substitution,
       resource availability, technical progress. In general pessimistic.
4.26 Sigurdson, J., 'Resources and the Environment in China', *Ambio.*
       Oslo, 1975, Vol 4, No 3, pp. 112.
4.27 Surrey, A. J. and Bromley, A. J., 'Energy Resources', in Cole *et al.*
       (1973), (*ref. 1.3*).
4.28 Sutolov, Alexander, *Minerals in World Affairs.* University of
       Utah, 1972.

4.29 Tooms, J. S., 'Potentially exploitable marine metals', *Endeavour*. Sept. 1970.

4.30 United Nations (1973), (*ref. 2.21*), Chapter 11; 'Population and natural resources'.

4.31 Valery, M., 'Place in the sun for Helium', *New Scientist*. 30th Nov. 1972.

4.32 Warren, Kenneth, *Mineral Resources*. Penguin, 1974.
A good general introduction to the subject.

4.33 Wells, F. J., *The Long Run Availability of Phosphorus*. Baltimore: John Hopkins University Press for Resources for the Future Inc, 1975.

4.34 Whitaker, John C., *Striking a Balance: Environment and Natural Resources Policy in the Nixon–Ford Years* (AEI–Hoover Policy Series). NY: American Enterprise Institute for Public Policy Research, 1976.

4.35 'The earth's resources: a new look, *Impact of Science on Society*, **XXIV**, (3), July–Sept. 1974 (whole issue).

4.36 *Science*, **191**, 20 Feb. 1976.
Whole issue on materials substitution and recycling.

4.37 Keyfitz, N., 'World Resources and the World Middle Class', *Scientific American*, **235**, (1), July 1976, pp. 28–35.

4.38 Radetzki, Marion, 'Where should developing countries' minerals be processed? The country view versus the multinational view', *World Development*, **5**, (4), Apr. 1977, pp. 325–34.

4.39 Tilton, J. E., 'The continuing debate over the exhaustion of non-fuel resources', *Natural Resources Forum*, **1**, (2), 1977, pp. 167–73.

JOURNALS

Natural Resources Journal.
Resources Policy.
Technology Review.

Points for discussion or essays

1. Discuss the definition of a 'non-renewable natural resource'. (*refs. 4.1, 4.5, 4.19*).
2. Do natural resources change in relation to time, technology and markets? If so, give examples. (*refs. 4.1, 4.4, 4.27*).
3. Discuss the relationship between technological progress and resources.

4. How do the materials we use today compare with those we used (a) fifty (b) one hundred (c) one thousand years ago? Under what circumstances will they change in the future?

5. Which would be the most significant constraints to resource availability in the future: physical and technological limits, or socio-political ones?

6. How much of each non-renewable resource do we need? In the previous chapter on food we saw that we have some idea of how many kilo-calories are needed per day for survival. Do we have an accurate idea of the limits of material needs: one car, two cars, a second home for everyone, washing machines? (*ref. 4.9*).

7. Is it reasonable to assume that, 'as the rest of the world develops economically, it will follow basically the US pattern of consumption — a sharp upward curve as output per capita grows, followed by a levelling off'? Discuss the basis for such an assumption. (*refs. 4.18, 4.E1, 4.E17, 4.30*).

8. Discuss the 'Balance of Nature' in relation to *The Limits to Growth* recommendations that we live in equilibrium with nature. Bearing in mind that the world is ultimately running out of resources, is it possible to live in complete harmony with Nature? What would be the implications for Western Society of living in complete harmony with Nature? Can we talk of a 'reasonable harmony'? (*refs. 4.2, 4.8, 4.17*).

9. *The Limits to Growth* does not discuss energy resources in any detail. What are the implications of energy demands upon the conclusions reached by *The Limits to Growth*? Are we at present experiencing problems in relation to demand or supply, or both? Are physical constraints dominant? At what rate should the oil in the North Sea be used? (*see Postscript on Energy*).

10. It is claimed that some materials such as helium, mercury, silver might eventually be depleted. Does this necessarily mean the collapse of the industrial system? (*refs. 4.1, 4.5, 4.6, 4.23, 4.27, 4.33*).

11. Population size is obviously one determinant of the total demand level for food, resources and so on. Total world demand for metals is estimated to have grown ten-fold between 1900 and 1970, while nearly twenty times as much non-metallic minerals (cement, chemicals, sand and gravel etc.) are now being used. On the other hand, world population slightly more than doubled over the same

period of time. Discuss, for food or minerals or anything else you prefer, the relative contribution to total demand which may stem from changes in population size or from other sources such as industrialization.
12. Discuss the merits and demerits of industrial civilization. Is it monolithic? (*refs. 1.4, 1.5, 1.8, 2.5, 3.7, 3.29, 4.8*).

Questions related to *Limits to Growth*

1. Discuss the role of natural resources in the *Limits* model. (The important point is whether it is critical in affecting the results of the model).
2. 'Within the static framework imposed by the assumptions of fixed techniques of energy production and finite reserves of particular forms of energy, exponential growth in energy consumption inevitably leads to the depletion of world resources'. Discuss this statement in relation to *Limits*.
3. Examine the *Limits* assertion that if current trends continue resources will be depleted. Have they considered all the trends?
4. In relation to resources Page has written:
   'The two key assumptions made in the World 3 Model are that, on aggregate, the world has 250 years supply of minerals (at current consumption rates) and that the economic cost of exploiting the remaining deposits will increase significantly'. Are these assumptions reasonable?
5. There are a further two key assumptions underlying the latter relationship (that economic costs of exploiting the remaining deposits will increase significantly).
   'Assumption 1: The capital costs of locating, extracting, processing and distributing, i.e. obtaining virgin natural resources, will rise as the resources are depleted.
   Assumption 2: The progress of technology will not be sufficient to counteract the effect of assumption 1 as the fraction of resources remaining approaches zero'.
   Discuss the viability of these assumptions.
6. What is a 'static index'?
7. Given the assumption of 250 years supply of resources is there any alternative to a slow down in industrial production at some time in the future? Discuss the implications of this assumption (a) upon the model output; (b) in relation to per capita resource use.

8. This chapter 'downplays too much the difference in consumption rates between the less developed countries and the industrial countries'. Discuss this opinion.

Postscript on Energy

Energy is treated in the MIT models as part of 'non-renewable resources'. While the availability and accessibility of non-renewable resources as a whole has been shown to be critical to the conclusions reached in *The Limits to Growth* (p. 73), energy resources are not dealt with in any detail.

The Limits to Growth was published in 1972. In the text above we have mentioned the action taken by OPEC in 1973 which precipitated the oil crisis in the industrialized countries. The effect upon oil prices caused by the bargaining power of OPEC — as opposed to a rise in prices due to a shortage of resources — has been mentioned. The emphasis upon energy in recent years has overshadowed the early seventies concern about pollution, and the advent of the oil crisis vividly illustrates the effect that the unforeseen can have upon projections into the future.

Two recent publications have reached conclusions which may be classified as 'optimistic' and 'guardedly optimistic'. In his chapter on energy Kahn (*ref. 4.E3*) concludes:

> Except for temporary fluctuations caused by bad luck or poor management, the world need not worry about energy shortages or costs in the future. And energy abundance is probably the world's best insurance that the entire human population (even 15–20 billion) can be well cared for, at least physically, during many centuries to come.

By contrast we have the more measured conclusions by Chesshire and Pavitt:

> ... provided the right policies are followed, it will be possible to avoid both the Malthusian trap of restraining world economic growth because of insufficient energy supplies and what some have even called a 'Faustian bargain' of a rapid and large-scale introduction of nuclear energy. Our preferred future would involve a continuous effort to improve energy conservation, most of all in North America, but also elsewhere in the industrially advanced world; an expansion in the production of coal, coupled with technical improvements related to its mining, transportation and use; a slow-down in the rate of expansion of

oil and natural gas production; a cautious and diversified exploration of nuclear reactor designs; the expansion of hydroelectric power; and the expansion of the unconventional sources of geothermal energy, and wind and solar power. An insurance policy against diminishing returns in energy investment will involve the maintenance of real energy prices at post-1973 levels, a growing contribution of the petrochemical industry towards improvements in coal-based technology, and a much more flexible and diversified pattern of investment by governments in energy R & D than has hitherto been the case.

Chesshire and Pavitt continue with the important proviso:

The achievement of these objectives will depend on the containment of the nuclear and electricity lobbies, and may be resisted by the automobile industry. It will also depend on compensating countries which are energy poor — and particularly those in South East Asia — for the increased costs of energy.

The central issues related to the energy question may be dealt with by consideration of the following questions and topics:

---

1. What are energy resources? (refs. 4.E2, 4.E3, 4.E8, 4.E22, 4.E23, 4.E32, 4.E36).
2. To what extent have major sources of energy altered?
   (a) since the Pharoahs?
   (b) during the last millenium in Europe?
   (c) over the last 200 years?
   (d) over the past 25 years?
   (refs. 4.E1, 4.E2, 4.E12, 4.E13, 4.E27, 4.E46).
3. Discuss the nature and extent of energy reserves. (refs. 4.E1, 4.E2, 4.E3).
4. What are the prospects and constraints upon nuclear energy from (a) fission (b) fusion? (refs. 4.E2, 4.E3, 4.E17, 4.E19, 4.E38, 4.E47, 4.E48).
5. Discuss the role played by science and technology in the exploitation of sources of energy. (refs. 4.E2, 4.E31).
6. What are the prospects for alternative sources of energy: (a) solar (b) wind (c) biogas (d) geothermal? (refs. 4.E6, 4.E10, 4.E21, 4.E25, 4.E26, 4.E28, 4.E29).
7. Discuss the relationship between economic growth and energy consumption. (refs. 4.E1, 4.E14, 4.E17).

---

8. Describe the present pattern of energy consumption in industrialized societies. What are the prospects for an alteration in these patterns of demand? (refs. *4.E1, 4.E2, 4.E11, 4.E24 4.E27, 4.E36*).
9. Write a brief history of the oil crisis in 1973 and its aftermath (refs. *4.E4, 4.E5, 4.E9, 4.E11, 4.E13, 4.E16, 4.E30, 4.E34*).
10. To what extent have consumption and the pattern of consumption been affected by the threefold price increase.
11. Discuss the basis of the argument that the rise in oil prices was as much a product of the long term plans of the oil companies, as a response to pressure by OPEC. (refs. *4.E4, 4.E5, 4.E9, 4.E16*).
12. Discuss the role of energy in developing countries. (ref. *4.E32*).

Reading

ESSENTIAL

4.E1 Chesshire, J. and Pavitt, K., 'Some energy futures'. Chapter 5 Freeman and Jahoda (eds.), (1978), (ref. *1.8*), pp. 113–168.

4.E2 Surrey, A. J. and Bromley, A. J., 'Energy resources', Chapter 8 in Cole *et al.*, (1973), (ref. *1.3*).

4.E3 Kahn *et al.*, 'Energy: exhaustible to inexhaustible', in Kahn *et al.*, (1977), (ref. *1.12*).

4.E4 Englers, Robert, *The Brotherhood of Oil: Energy Policy and the Public Interest.* Univ. of Chicago Press, 1977.

4.E5 Sampson, Anthony, *The Seven Sisters: The Great Oil Companies and the World they shaped.* Viking, 1975.

ADDITIONAL

4.E6 Alward, R. *et al.*, *A Handbook of Appropriate Technology.* Ottawa: Canadian Hunger Foundation, 1976.

4.E7 *Directory of International Energy Statistics* (IES Co) (Po Box 666, Washington DC 20044).

4.E8 *Energy Global Prospects 1985–2000.* Report of the workshop on alternative energy strategies (WAES). NY: McGraw Hill, 1977.

4.E9   Barraclough, G., 'The great world crisis I', *New York Review of Books*, **21**, (21 & 22), 23 Jan. 1975, pp. 20–29. Continued 7 Aug. 1975 pp. 23–30 and 13 May 1976 pp. 31–41

Articles which survey much of the literature on food and energy.

4.E10   Boyle, Godfrey and Harper, Peter (ed.), *Radical Technology*. Wildwood House, 1976.

4.E11   Chapman, P., *Fuel's Paradise*. Penguin, 1975.

4.E12   Cipolla, C., *The Economic History of World Population*. Penguin, 1974, pp. 33–62.

4.E13   Commoner, B., *The Poverty of Power: Energy and the Economic Crisis*. NY: Knopf, 1976.

4.E14   Darmstadter, J., *Energy in the World Economy*. Baltimore: John Hopkins Press, 1971.

4.E15   Eckholm, Eric, *The other energy crisis: Firewood*. Washington: Worldwatch, 1975.

4.E16   Ellis, Frank (ed.), *Oil and Development*. Bulletin of the Institute of Development Studies (Univ. of Sussex) Special Issue, *Vol 6*, No 2, Oct. 1974.

4.E17   Foley, G., *The Energy Question*. Penguin, 1976.

4.E18   Francis, John and Abrecut, Paul, *Facing up to Nuclear Power: Risks and Potentialities of the large-scale use of nuclear energy*. Philadelphia PA: Westminster Press, 1976.

4.E19   Foreman, H. (ed.), *Nuclear Power and the Public*. Univ. of Minnesota, 1970.

4.E20   Hayes, Denis, *Energy: the Case for Conservation*. Washington DC: Worldwatch, 1976.

4.E21   Hayes, Denis, *Energy: the Solar Prospect*. Washington DC: Worldwatch, 1977.

4.E22   Hinton, C., 'World sources of energy in the late twentieth century', reprinted in Open University, *Power and Society*. Technology Foundation Course – The Man made world, Units 20–21, Appendix I.

4.E23   Holdren, J. and Herrerra, P., *Energy: a Crisis in Power*. San Francisco: Sierra Club, 1971.

4.E24   Illich, I. D., *Energy and Equity*. Calder and Boyers, 1974.

4.E25   Jequier, N. (ed.), *Appropriate Technology: Problems and Promises*. Paris: OECD, 1976.

4.E26   Kenwood, M., *Potential Energy: An Analysis of World Energy Technology*. CUP, 1976.

4.E27   Leach, G., *The Motor Car and Natural Resources*. Paris: OECD, 1972.

4.E28   Lovins, A. B., *Soft Energy Paths: Towards a Durable Peace*. Cambridge Mass.: Ballinger, 1977.

4.E29   Lovins, A. B., *World Energy Strategies: Facts issues and Options*. Earth Resources Research Ltd for Friends of the Earth, 1973.

4.E30 Mackay, D. and Mackay, G. A., *Political Economy of North Sea Oil*. Martin Robertson, 1975.

4.E31 Maddox, J., *Beyond the Energy Crisis*. McGraw Hill, 1975.

4.E32 Makhihani, A. and Poole, A., *Energy and Agriculture in the Third World*. Cambridge Mass.: Ballinger, 1975.

4.E33 Makhihani, A., *Energy Policy for the Rival Third World*. London: International Institute for Environment and Development, 1976.

4.E34 Odell, P. R., *Oil and World Power: Background to the Oil Crisis*. Penguin, 1974.

4.E35 Odum, Howard T. and Odum, Elisabeth C., *Energy basis for Man and Nature*. McGraw Hill, 1976.

4.E36 Open University, *Energy Resources: The Earth's Physical Resources Block 3*. Open University, 1973.

4.E37 O'Toole, James and the University of Southern California Center for Futures Research, *Energy and Social Change*. Cambridge Mass: MIT Press, 1976.

4.E38 Patterson, W. C., *Nuclear Power*. Penguin, 1976.

4.E39 Pimentel, D. *et al.*, 'Food production and the energy crisis', *Science*, **182**, (1973), pp. 443–449.
        Discusses the efficiency of agriculture with respect to energy.

4.E40 Stone, I. F., 'War for oil?', *New York Review of Books*, **22**, (1), Feb. 1975, pp. 7–10.

4.E41 'How shall we conserve energy?', *Technology Review*, **76**, (5), Mar.–Apr. 1974 (whole issue).

4.E42 *Technology Review*, **78**, (4), Feb. 1976, special issue on offshore oil.

4.E43 '6 views of atomic energy', *Bull. of Atomic Scientists*, **33**, (3), Mar. 1977, pp. 59–69.

4.E44 Barrie, T. W. and Leslie, D., 'Energy Policy in developing countries', *Energy Policy*, **6**, (2), June 1978, pp. 119–128.

4.E45 Caudle, P. G., 'Chemicals and Energy: the next 25 years', *Futures*, **10**, (5), Oct. 1978, pp. 361–379.

4.E46 Jevons, W. Stanley, 'The coal question – can Britain survive?', *Environment and Change*, **2**, (6), Feb. 1974, pp. 373–80.

4.E47 Surrey, J. and Hugget, C., 'Opposition to nuclear power: a review of international experience', *Energy Policy*, **4**, (4), Dec. 1976.

4.E48 Wonder, E. F., 'Decision making and reorganisation of the British nuclear power industry', *Research Policy*, **5**, (3), July 1976, pp. 240–68.

JOURNALS

Energy Digest.

Energy Policy.

New Scientist – Energy File (weekly).

Research Policy.

Chapter Five
Pollution

'Pollution' has been a dirty word for some time now. For many years
the smoking chimneys of factories were the symbols of progress,
development and, perhaps above all, opportunity: 'where there's
muck there's brass'. But the hue and cry of the last few years has had
a profound effect on public attitudes towards such symbols. Now
smoking chimneys are liable to raise images of smog, diseases of the
lung and a rampant technology that overrides the needs of human
beings for fresh air and clean water.

This change of attitude to pollution over a relatively short period
of time shows, perhaps somewhat unexpectedly, that the definition of
pollution is not necessarily clear-cut. The anthropologist and philosopher, Mary Douglas, has written at length upon this subject and one
of her most intriguing examples is the case of two African tribes living
alongside one another in the same habitat, whose ideas concerning what
is pollution and what is not are diametrically opposed. These remarks
as to the possibility of radically different conceptions of 'pollution'
and their implications are only intended to indicate the possible breadth
of the subject. In this chapter our definition of pollution will be far
more mundane: matter and physical processes in the wrong place.

In the right place, and in the right quantity, the substance may be
not only harmless but beneficial: consider the treatment of cancer by
radioactive methods and the effect of fertilizer and pesticides in a field
upon the size and quality of the crop produced. The substances or
processes may be in the 'wrong' place in three different senses. Firstly,
it may be wrong 'aesthetically' in something like the original sense of
the word: displeasing to the senses. Secondly, the substance or process in
that place in a certain quantity may be dangerous to human health, or
may eventually move into places in which it will be dangerous. Thirdly,
the substances or processes may destroy wild life — both animals and
plants.

In general, we will not be discussing aesthetic pollution except in so
far as it is a by-product of the others. The relationship between man
and wild life is a complex one. According to Barry Commoner one of
the first principles of ecology is that everything is related to everything
else. As such, while the links between man and wildlife are not immediately apparent, they exist, and the web of life is such that with the
collapse of wildlife would come the collapse of man. The authors of
the *Blueprint for Survival* stated this succinctly: 'Homo sapiens himself
depends on the continued resilience of those ecological networks of
which eagles and primroses are integral parts'. But it is debatable as to
the extent to which this is true and the extent to which the by-products

of man's activities are eradicating other flora and fauna. In respect to the latter many animals became extinct before the appearance of man and the depradation of species by man is much more clearly related to direct assaults upon them — by means of gun, trap and fishing net — than by industrial poisoning by air and water. It is far easier to see the extent to which man is dependent upon the air he breathes, the water he drinks and the plant and animal foods he eats. If this aspect of man's web of life is corrupted he is in immediately recognizable danger. We shall therefore concentrate upon pollution as it affects man directly either by air, water or food. The wider relationships between man and his environment with a full treatment of ecology may be found in a SISCON publication *Science and the Environment — Unit One* by Worboys, Marstrand and Lowe.

Solving the problem of pollution then, means reducing the flow of substances or processes into places which are 'wrong'. To achieve this one must 'first know what substances are in fact harmful and by what means and in what quantity they produce their deleterious effects'. We will address these questions by considering three types of pollution which have received widespread attention. We have chosen these particular three because of their global dimensions and potency: thermal pollution, DDT and air pollution.

Thermal pollution

Robert Heilbroner, the noted American economist, wrote in his recent essay *The Human Prospect* that 'One barrier confronts us with all the force of an ultimatum from nature. It is that all industrial production, including, of course, the extraction of resources, requires the use of energy, and that all energy, including that generated from natural processes such as wind, power or solar radiation, is inextricably involved with the emission of heat'.

It has been estimated that 'Present emission of energy is about 1/15000 of the absorbed solar flux. But if the present rate of growth continued for 250 years emissions would reach 100% of the absorbed solar flux. The resulting increase in the earth's temperature would be about $50°C$ — a condition totally unsuitable for human habitation'. But the temperature of the atmosphere is not only raised by direct emission of heat. Carbon dioxide released during the burning of fossil fuels acts in such a way as to absorb sunlight that would normally be reflected back into space. This 'greenhouse effect' compounds the effect of direct heat emission.

Many apocalyptic scenarios have been deduced by such an increase in thermal pollution, perhaps the most widely used being the melting of the polar ice-caps and the consequent elimination of major cities of the world by a 60—100 foot increase in sea-level.

However, there is another process that counteracts the increase in atmospheric temperature. The amount of the solar flux which reaches the earth is affected by the amount of dust in the atmosphere. The more dust, the more solar flux is reflected and therefore the less heat which reaches the earth i.e. the higher the earth's reflectivity or *albedo*. Industrial activity and transportation (particularly stratospheric jet transport) are seen to contribute significantly to atmospheric dust concentration. Several other scenarios have been drawn based on a radical decrease in atmospheric temperature caused by industrial activity — the most common being the precipitation of the next ice age.

At the same time, volcanic activity is also a major source of atmospheric particulate matter — the eruption of a volcano on the island of Bali in 1963 is now known to have produced more dust in the upper atmosphere than had been there before: the temperature of the upper atmosphere almost immediately increased by six to eight degrees centigrade, showing that extra amounts of energy from the sun were being absorbed high in the atmosphere, consequently less was reaching the earth. These effects were still apparent in the late sixties when temperatures in the upper atmosphere were still well above normal and too high to be accounted for by industrial activity.

In the face of all the extra heat and carbon dioxide that has been pumped into the atmosphere since 1940 the average temperatures appear to have declined slightly since that time. This has been seen as a justification for the view of increased atmospheric turbidity. Well it might be, but to what extent is it the result of industrial activity? We have already seen the dramatic effect of one volcanic explosion — and the conclusion of another MIT report (which was sceptical of the effects of man's activities) was that man introduces fewer particles into the atmosphere than enter from natural sources. Further, other scientists have argued that the overall cyclic behavior of the earth's climatic patterns override the influences of either the heating or cooling effects of pollutant activities.

Thermal pollution is, when we look at it carefully, too complicated to pronounce on glibly. Local perturbations in, for example, the water discharged from a reactor or in the atmosphere around a big industrial area, may have serious ill-effects on our environments; in our concern with the global we must not lose sight of these. As touched on earlier, once man's production of energy totals a significant fraction of the absorbed solar flux, the present delicate balance between incident energy and reflected energy plus radiated energy will shift; radiated energy will increase. For this to happen the temperature of the earth's radiating surface will have to rise and this will have major repercussions. The sensitivity of this energy balance we do not know. How much can it be disturbed before the effects on the environment become serious? Will this point be reached in 500 years or 100 years? Cyclic variations in the atmosphere occur naturally and are large enough to hide any effect man's activities may yet have had. In consequence experimental confirmation of any predicted changes is, as yet, impossible to obtain. All this adds up to uncertainty; we have no reason to panic but, equally, we cannot afford to be complacent.

DDT

Until 1962 DDT was universally acknowledged as one of the enormous benefits that progress in science and technology had given to man: an undisputed blessing. In 1962 Rachel Carson wrote *Silent Spring* which vividly described the detrimental side-effects of pesticides and the even greater dangers which lay in store for man by its continued and increased use. Since that time a voluminous quantity of material has been produced about the insecticide — we will touch upon a few of the issues involved.

DDT was first used widely in the mid-forties and its effect upon the reduction of malaria throughout the world was almost instantaneous. At the same time its devastating effect upon crop pests resulted in much higher harvests. Since that time the quantities used throughout the world have sky-rocketed. Some time later the first deleterious side-effects became apparent: Firstly, resistant strains of pest were selected. As the insecticide had already killed off the natural predators, and as pests usually bred faster once the DDT resistant strains of insects had developed, there were no longer enough natural predators to keep them in check so pest populations bloomed again and harvests shrank. Secondly, DDT was seen to be extremely mobile and insoluble in water so it spread throughout the globe especially in the oceans. Thirdly, DDT was seen to have a deleterious effect upon certain species of bird. Fourthly, although insoluble in water it is soluble in fat and higher concentrations of DDT are reported in the fat of human tissue. Finally, it was considered to be persistent, i.e. it was thought not to degrade to harmless constituents.

Among the replies to such arguments have been the following. Insecticides can be divided into two classes, 'those which cause resistance in populations of pests which are not entirely exterminated and those which are entirely unaffected', and the occasional outbreaks of new DDT-resistant pests does not cause as much damage as the amount of food saved by the use of DDT in the first place. Another variation on the theme that the benefits to man outweigh the disbenefits, applies to the diminution of certain species of bird. Man is seen as having priority — 'Not all people are satisfied that the life of a pelican has the same value as that of a human being which might be saved from an insect-carried disease'. As to the persistence of DDT, particularly in the oceans (and thus to its mobility and global distribution), it is argued that within forty days of entering the ocean only 7% of the original pesticide remains intact, the rest having been broken down into harmless constituents. Finally, the presence of DDT in human tissue has not increased over the last twenty years. More importantly, however, even an avowedly anti-DDT article (in De Twyler (1971) *ref. 3.12*) stated 'No reliable study has yet revealed a causal association between the presence of these residues and human disease'. Also it has been pointed out that it is only in the USA and perhaps Sweden that DDT has been used recklessly by the ton without heed to what will happen to the DDT which falls where it is not needed. [Films have graphically captured the sight of pesticides being sprayed from an aeroplane and drenching agricultural workers as they labor under the California sun]. 'The question seems to be not whether chemical pesticides should be used at all, but whether they need to be thrown around by the ton from squadrons of aircraft'.

Air pollution

' "The air nimbly and sweetly recommends itself unto our gentle senses". So wrote William Shakespeare in *Macbeth*. Would a poet of comparable skill living in a modern city be likely to express a similar sentiment?' This is a prime example of intellectual sleight of hand. Ehrlich implies that conditions in Shakespeare's time were much cleaner than now and therefore the extent to which matters have deteriorated. Long before the reign of Elizabeth I the problem had appeared and been recognized in English towns. The earliest known record of an attempt to prevent air pollution in England dates back to 1273 when an ordinance was issued, prohibiting the use of coal in London as being 'prejudicial to health'. In 1306 a royal proclamation prohibited the use of coal by artificers in their furnaces. By Elizabeth I's reign the situation in London had worsened considerably and she is reported to have complained that smoke issuing from breweries in the vicinity of the palace caused her 'grievous annoyance' and towards the end of her reign the use of coal was prohibited in London while Parliament was sitting. As well as this aspect of air pollution, many accounts of the towns of the middle-ages refer to the stench from open sewers — with present-day connotations of dangers other than those resulting from air pollution itself. In addition, the use of the opening quote implies that the actor was referring to the smell of a city whereas in fact he was referring to the countryside — the Scottish countryside at that.

Ehrlich himself has discussed the difficulty of assessing the hazards of air pollution. Among these difficulties are '(1) Pollutants are numerous and varied, many of them are difficult to detect. Their consequences vary geographically. In many areas techniques for monitoring pollutants are inadequate, and long term records are unavailable . . . (2) It is usually impossible to determine with precision the degree of exposure of a given individual to specific pollutants; (3) Degree of air pollution is correlated with other factors, such as degree of exposure to various kinds of stress, other kinds of pollution and food additives. Such factors must be considered in data analysis'.

The industrial centers in the USA and Western Europe are seen as the greatest sources of global air pollution. It is, however, acknowledged that in the USA air pollution is concentrated over cities. Smog reduces the amount of sunlight reaching New York and Chicago by 25 and 40% respectively. This raises doubts as to the extent to which air pollution from industrial sources is a global problem and not a local one. Global issues are so much more intractable than doorstep issues which are open to modification by local political action. At the same time it has been estimated that in the USA 70% of the pollutants in the atmosphere above urban and industrial areas found their way into the air through automobile exhausts (75–80% in Los Angeles). The authors of *The Limits to Growth* built into their model that air pollution increases with industrial output and population growth. Yet Beckmann (*ref. 2.5*) argues that *even* in the USA the figures over recent years show a decrease of air pollution from the biggest culprit – the motor car. Such being the case, is the situation as critical in countries which do not have the same concentration of cars per acre as in the USA?

Similar types of arguments and controversies surround a host of other pollutants from sulfur dioxide or radioactivity to the side-effects of monoculture. Several generalized questions can, however, be drawn from the above discussion of only three types of pollution:

1. Is it possible, on a global scale, to identify which man-made pollutants are increasing at an exponential rate and faster than the air and oceans can break them down into harmless substances? The authors of *The Limits to Growth* state confidently 'virtually every pollutant that has been measured as a function of time appears to be increasing exponentially'. But it should be pointed out that on the previous page they had written 'The *few kinds* of pollution that actually have been measured over time seem to be increasing exponentially' – which puts a slightly different complexion to the first statement. This question involves the monitoring of pollution: the identification, isolation and measurement of pollutants over time. Monitoring pollutants is affected by the difficulty of defining natural unpolluted levels – this difficulty is enhanced by the cyclical nature of climatic variations and the additives injected from natural sources.

2. Do we have sufficient evidence to show cause and effect relationships between the pollutants and the harmful effects in man? Does this evidence justify the *Limits to Growth* assumption that 'an increase in global pollution by a factor of 10 would have a great

effect?' Here we are involved with questions related to the norms from which to measure the effects of pollution.

3. Do we have evidence that the benefits given by scientific and industrial advance are outweighed by the disbenefits arising out of unexpected side-effects? Are these disbenefits sufficient to conclude that industrial activity of any kind should stop immediately?

4. Is there a man-made global crisis? When one considers that a natural activity such as thunderstorm unleashes the energy of several hundred hydrogen bombs does this give pause for thought? The conclusion of another MIT report *Man's Impact on the Global Environment* was that 'in reality man does intervene, because he can without intending to do so reach some leverage points in the system'. Is pollution one of them?

5. Does the removal of any historical perspective on the problem of pollution lead to the feeling that it has never happened before and therefore that this is a threat with which man has no means of coping? Is this exacerbated by focussing upon the trends of substances that have only recently been introduced into the environment and even more recently recognized as dangerous?

6. Is pollution primarily a global or a localized problem?
Many authors have concluded from the evidence they have surveyed that global disruption is imminent and that the thalidomide and Minimata Bay disasters and the petro-chemical smog over Los Angeles are but early manifestations of that disruption. However, the conclusions of the authors of *Thinking about the Future* are that all the questions are debatable, the balance of opinion being that there is no global threat to man. But they assert that there are clearly local occurrences, particularly near cities or areas which are intensely farmed or where manufacturing takes place (especially within the manufacturing establishment itself), that are potentially or actually extremely harmful to man. One of the chief faults of alarmist conclusions such as those drawn by Ehrlich and the authors of *The Limits to Growth* is that by crying *wolf* over the global nature of pollution they will prejudice the chances of local occurrences being taken seriously:

> This reliance upon the trends of a few years could result in misuse of the speculations based on the model either to frighten people into taking hasty action, as in the case of substituting NTA for phosphorus in detergents [which had disastrous results], or to discredit the study and, by implication, the legitimate concern for resources and the environment which it expresses.
> . . . By aggregating all pollutants and assuming that they behave in some composite way, attention is drawn away from what are urgent and still soluble problems and diverted into speculation upon an imaginary race against time between 'life' and 'global asphyxiation'.

So far we have discussed the pollutants in the context of an assessment of both the extent to which they are present in the atmosphere, water or land (monitoring), and the extent to which they damage man or the plants and animals upon which man depends (norms). While the debate rages as to the answer to these problems on a global scale, it can hardly be denied that incidents such as thalidomide, the Minimata Bay, factory processing or methods of work, such as welding and coal mining, and the Los Angeles smog have taken place or are on a continuing reality which present serious threats to humans who are in the area where these polluting activities have taken place. As such there exists a very real social need to limit these activities, if not to eliminate them. Two major aspects arise as soon as we begin to discuss this question of the control of pollution. In order to control pollution we have first to identify from where that pollution emanates, i.e. the cause. Once we have identified the causes we can begin to discuss methods of control.

Causes of pollution

'People are pollution' says Ehrlich. We have seen this phrase in the chapter on population and it rears its ugly head again here. People are seen by many writers on the environmental crisis as the prime cause of pollution. For example Lamont Cole has said:

> Many of the most important problems currently facing man are ecological problems arising from the unrestrained growth of the human population and the resultant increasing strains being placed on the earth's life support system.

A common way in which this argument is expanded upon is as follows: throughout the industrialized world the air, water and solid pollution per person is increasing at a great rate; the population of the world is increasing as well; the population of the world will get steadily richer over the next few decades; their patterns of consumption and waste production will increase in the same way as has developed in the industrialized world — reference is made to the demands by people for an increased supply of consumer goods. From this sequence has been drawn 'Hardin's Law': Population times prosperity equals pollution.

The equation of people with pollution is challenged. The rate of population growth in the industrialized countries is low and, relatively speaking, widespread pollution has only recently been identified as a serious problem. As measures are already being taken to limit pollution it is unwise to extrapolate the trends of the past few decades into the distant future. In the developing countries, although the populations are growing very fast, their production of pollution per person is very small by comparison with that of the United States in particular — it has been estimated that fifty times the strain on the environment is induced by the birth of an American child than by an Indian one — in other words, the level of waste in a country which is not yet industrialized and does not yet rely to the same extent on consumer goods, is much lower. Furthermore, if the world does become richer there is no inevitability about its pattern of consumption following that of the US, and even if it relies to a great extent on consumer goods there is no certainty that it will follow the US pattern of built-in obsolescence and superfluous packaging. While acknowledging that within Western culture certain patterns of demand for goods are held to exist, these are not seen as being an inevitable human result of increased material standards of living. Indeed, at the time of the UN Conference on the Human Environment in 1972, it was widely believed that the Third World would not take environmental problems seriously because they would press for industrial advances regardless of the side-effects of pollution. But the experience of the United Nations Environment Programme since then has belied this view.

These arguments against the correlation of people with pollution blend easily into the second major cause of pollution: the social system itself. This may perhaps be best introduced by two examples from the USA. It has been estimated that over 50% of the air pollution in the US is caused by the motor car. Secondly, many of the nation's cattle are kept under conditions which are the bovine equivalent of the battery chicken. The cattle sewage produced from these farms feeds directly into the same sewerage system as that for humans. It has been estimated that half the sewage in the States is from cattle. Material which is potentially good, natural, self-distributing fertilizer not only exerts a stress on the constructed domestic sewerage system but it also becomes an eventual contributor to river and sea water pollution. Neither of these two examples of pollutant source are inevitable, they result from the particular way in which the American society has developed, and even in that system they have developed during a time when pollution was not considered a serious problem. A society which sets less store by individual transport immediately limits the amount of air pollution at present generated by the internal combustion engine. It has been said that if the production and consumption of unnecessary commodities were limited then pollution would decline. But here we meet the sticky definition of a 'necessary product' which is one step away from the extremely difficult problem of distinguishing between 'wants' and 'needs'. A simpler way of approaching this problem in relation to pollution (which skirts the issue of 'wants' and 'needs') is through the question 'How much pollution is a society prepared to bear for the things it considers necessary to produce?'

Although we will not attempt to answer this question directly, it is crucial to an understanding of the relationship between pollution and the social system.

Several writers, while seeing the fundamental cause of pollution as related to the social system have identified capitalist society as being the major source of the present crisis. They have stated that only in socialist systems is it possible to obtain pollution free societies. Other writers have demonstrated that the industrialized socialist countries also have pollution problems. While industrialized socialist countries have also experienced pollution problems, it would seem that with their moral outlook of better social welfare for all, the centralized methods of control could result in a better environment for the average man and better systems of a control once a pollution problem is identified. The limitation to such an assertion would occur if the industrialized socialist country were to pursue quantity of production regardless of the ill effects on people. Regardless of the social system it would appear that the onus should not be on the people to prove the damage created by an industry but on the industry to show that it is not harming the people.

The third major cause of pollution is seen as technology. In some cases this has come through the consideration of difficulties experienced by both the major forms of industrialized society — capitalist and socialist — and the identification of both systems' reliance upon technology. In the main, however, it seems to have come from the recent appearance of several disruptive side-effects of technology which have been generalized into a broad attack upon technology itself.

> Technology, while creating a 'better life' for man, has created more environmental changes per capita, thus escalating man's impact. Also technology yearly becomes a more and more powerful tool, amplifying our ability to change nature . . . Technological advance has furthermore spurred urbanization, with its especially intensive impacts.

While Barry Commoner, the famous ecologist, has said:

> Technology, therefore, powerfully amplifies the effect of human beings on the biosphere . . . technology has introduced into the biosphere substances wholly new to it.

He continues to say that the prevalent view is that environmental deterioration is a consequence of relatively minor faults in our technology — the lack of adequate scrubbers on smokestacks; insufficient treatment of sewage; the absence of proper fume traps on motor car exhausts. Commoner insists that the environmental deterioration experienced is not due to minor faults but to major ones. He gives examples of sewage treatment, fertilizer application, improved performance in the internal combustion engine and insecticide treatment, where the advances in technological capability to achieve the desired end, whether better sewage treatment or a higher performance engine, resulted in greater pollution. The analysis is extended to suggest that technology, by interfering with and altering the constituents of the biosphere, for example photosynthesis, is self-destructive — 'our most advanced technology will come to naught and any economic and political system which depends on it will founder'. Commoner concludes:

> Modern technology has so stressed the web of processes in the living environment at its most vulnerable points that there is little leeway left in the system.

Many other writers agree with Commoner. Such an identification of technology as a major cause of pollution is elaborately expanded upon in *The Careless Technology*. As one of the writers in that volume concluded:

> I think it is becoming increasingly clear that technology by its very nature must cause problems. It consists in substituting a man-devised organization of matter, the 'technosphere', which is relatively crude and geared to the satisfaction of short-term anthropocentric ends, for the 'biosphere', remarkable for its subtlety and geared to the maintenance of long-term stability, i.e. survival.

Certainly science and technology have opened the way for the use of larger amounts of energy and major sources of pollution do stem from the various ways in which men use energy — ranging from the oil lost during transportation, and exhaust fumes from motor cars to the radioactive wastes from nuclear power stations. But is it reasonable to subscribe to the view that 'technology by its very nature must cause problems.? Do we never gain more on the swings than on the round-a-bouts? Are we really dealing with an 'inherently' polluting technology? If so, has man been damned since Prometheus stole the fire and man first smelted iron? Or are we in need of careful and sophisticated analysis of the meaning of technology and its role in society? Can it perhaps, as in the case of population, be linked to the social system in which that technology is located?

Questions as to the 'inherent' bias of science have been more fully explored by Brian Easlea in his book *Liberation and the Aims of Science*. However, one of the ways of tackling such an important topic would be by careful and sophisticated analysis aimed at understanding the dynamics of technology and its role in society. But even in the same articles by the two virulently anti-technology writers mentioned above, we find some indication of an answer to these questions. Commoner mentions at one point 'our technology *as it is currently construed* forms an intrinsically unstable relationship with the biosphere', and Edward Goldsmith somewhat ambivalently ends his peroration against technology by saying 'are the experiences described incriminating *"careless"* technology or technology itself when practised on a sufficient scale?' Although his rhetoric is against technology, he shows the possibility of construing it as 'careless' and the phrase 'practised on a sufficient scale' indicates a distinct social dimension to technology: technology is a product of society and as such it is amenable to control by that society.

It is thus possible to argue at an abstract level about the inevitability of population, technology or a social system being the major cause of pollution. Equally, it can be easily seen that such differing views of causes will lead to radically different views as to the means to be employed to limit or control pollution.

Those who see population as the major cause of the problem will seek to institute controls against the proliferation of people. If they see these problems in critical terms then they are especially likely to see solutions by authoritarian methods as the only ones by which to save mankind from a grisly future. Equally, for those who see the modern industrial state as the major cause and technology either as its willing but misguided handmaiden, or its evil generator, there will again be a spectrum of solutions varying from tampering with the system — and improving, by modification, the technology — to over-throwing the whole lot and returning *sans* tools to the primitive. Their attitude to control of pollution depends upon their position in that spectrum. The presuppositions which guide an analysis may also prejudice a valuational attitude. The issues raised by these questions of control in relation to causes are very close to the realm of politics and we will return to some of them in the next chapter.

It is thus possible to consider that the root causes of pollution stem from a particular social system (or increasing population or industrial technology), and to think that some solution to the pollution problem might result from a reorganization of such a social system (or a decrease in population or the complete redesigning of industrial technology). At the same time it must be recognized that these are large issues.

In the meantime, it might be possible to identify certain sources of pollution — such as the exhaust fumes of cars, the chimney stacks of power stations and the effluent pipes of a factory — and recognize that it is necessary to begin tackling such problems. Even the somewhat pessimistic MIT Report *Man's Impact on the Global Environment* concluded:

> It should be noted that the existence of a global problem does not imply the necessity for a global solution. The sources of

pollution are activities of men that can often be effectively controlled or regulated where they occur.

Attention to such lowly manifestations of pollution can still involve difficult questions related to control.

Control of pollution

In our society much concern has been expressed at the mention of control. It is seen, by some, as just another point at which the freedom of the individual or company is limited by central authority. It is held, by defenders of *laissez faire*, that internal economic considerations will compel the individuals or companies to limit their polluting capabilities: they will recognize that by impairing the quality of air and water in general they will ultimately be impairing their own ability to exist as a viable commercial enterprise. As such no controls are necessary.

In opposition to this standpoint others have written that most enterprises are only interested in short term gain and thus their concern about possible future damage to the environment is minimal. They see that such an attitude combined with the ill-effects of a runaway technology means that neither internal controls nor social controls such as legislation to control pollution will limit pollution. Such pessimism as to the weakness of social controls has led both to the *Limits to Growth* predictions of collapse through asphyxiation and to arguments for the institution of an immediate absolute clampdown on pollution: 'no pollution whatsoever'. In *Thinking About the Future*, Sinclair wrote:

> An essential assumption of the MIT work is that industrial growth and capital investment necessarily carry with them an inevitable and increasing pollution penalty. This view is explicitly justified by the assumption that social control mechanisms will be too little, too ineffective and too late to diminish hazards significantly.

But on the one hand institutionalized central control (control by government) of pollution does not offend internal structures of Western society or the freedom of the individual. Passmore has written that harming one's neighbor has long been seen as an evil to be resisted and that control over such actions has long been vested with a central authority.

On the other hand the question is whether those who advocate an immediate halting of all polluting industrial activities are justified in assuming that social control mechanisms will be 'too little, too ineffective and too late'.

Sinclair conducted an historical survey of the ways in which the British have coped with the problem of pollution during the last two hundred years. With respect to air pollution he concluded modestly that 'local situations as unacceptable as those of today have existed in the past and have been dealt with more or less successfully' and therefore considered that 'this review of previous situations has demonstrated the capability of the technological system to respond to social and administrative pressures effectively applied'.

But a colleague, Pauline Marstrand, is more forceful:

> Sinclair argues that, in general, England was a far messier place a hundred or two years ago than it is today, in spite of the presently far higher levels of production. He also shows that the introduction of anti-pollution legislation has had valuable effects in reducing the apparent absolute levels of pollution, while permitting increased production, and society's ability to impose social controls to reduce industrial externalities (including pollution), has improved, though perhaps unevenly, since the 19th century.

For example, the air in London is cleaner today than it was 22 years ago when a smog killed 4000 people; twenty years ago only eels could live in the lower Thames, now the river is the habitat of fifteen varieties of fish. These changes have been the direct result of legislation to limit pollution.

Elsewhere Sinclair has argued that this process of social control is still continuing:

> The first reports of the Royal Commission on Environmental Pollution (1971 and 1972) and of the US Council on Environmental Quality make it clear that many of the more obvious hazards and disamenities are being dealt with; the levels are being reduced, economic measures of various types are being brought into operation to deal with pollution.

And the MIT report *Man's Impact on the Global Environment* listed twenty three federal acts already in existence that relate to environmental concerns and pollution control. The political and legislative context is already prepared to cope with environmental problems.

At the same time, in the USA, an investigation into the effectiveness of new pollution controls on motor vehicles has graphically claimed that the controls are not worth the paper on which they are printed. Others have commented that certain industrial concerns are so powerful that it will be impossible to enforce the legislation that does exist. They claim that the very difficulty of identifying, isolating and monitoring pollution means that such industries will always be able to find legal loopholes in the legislation and thus avoid prosecution and the introduction of non-polluting methods. In the short term this may be true. But then we are no longer talking of pollution that is the inevitable product of runaway technology; if captains of industry are employing legal advice to ensure that they can continue to pollute, this is pollution by particular men. Sinclair has shown that faced with comparable situations in the past, society has responded successfully and new social controls are already being instituted against the present dangers.

Methods of control

Ironically it has been seen by some that 'more, not less, science and technology is needed to eliminate pollution and to clean up the environment'. These methods are seen to be needed to curb, cure and monitor pollution.

One of the most frequently advocated methods is that of 'Emissions Control'. 'As a point of departure for taking action, we recommend a principle of presumptive "source" responsibility . . . if something goes wrong it should be traced to its origin and corrected in terms of its cause, in part on a hypothesis that the source, protosource, or secondary source will typically be in the best position to take corrective measures, whether alone or with help from others; and in part on the view that the remedies available, the criteria for choice among them, and the implications of remedial action can best be appraised at the sources here defined'. This solution, while simple in concept and direct in action, raises questions as to how those responsible for the 'sources' should be made to institute controls and who should pay for the cost of these controls. Answers have been that those responsible for pollution 'sources' should be heavily taxed to induce improved methods of production, and that the consumer should be prepared to pay for the cost of reducing pollution. As to the 'polluter pays' principle it has been argued that the costs (resulting from taxation and pollution reducing equipment) would be passed immediately to the consumer, transforming the 'polluter pays' into the 'consumer pays' principle.

In relation to physical means of reducing pollution there is now a large inventory of mechanisms. These vary from the ingenious solution that the outflow pipe of a factory should be positioned upstream from its inflow pipe to the recycling of waste materials and obsolete products.

Conclusion

Passmore's prescription for coping with pollution: 'a successful attack on pollution involves the solution of a great variety of problems not only scientific and technological but moral, political, economic and administrative. We ought not to pretend to know the solution to a pollution problem until we know how to reduce the incidence of that form of pollution by the use of a method the costs of which are not greater than the resulting benefits, which is politically feasible, and which can be effectively administered without intolerable disadvantages, economic or social'.

Reading

ESSENTIAL

5.1   Marstrand, P. K. and Sinclair, T. C., 'The pollution sub-system', Chapter 7 in Cole *et al.* (1973) (*ref. 1.3*), pp. 80–89.
5.2   Sinclair, T. C., 'Environmentalism', Chapter 12 in Cole *et al.* (1973) (*ref. 1.3*), pp. 175–191.
5.3   Passmore, 'Pollution', Chapter 3 in Passmore (1974) (*ref. 2.4*), pp. 43–72.
5.4   Meadows *et al.* (1972) (*ref. 1.1*), pp. 69–86, 117–120.

ADDITIONAL

5.5   Beckermann (1974) (*ref. 3.7*).
      Chapter 5: 'Economic growth and pollution',
      Chapter 6: 'Pollution policy and the price mechanism',
      Chapter 7: 'The economic burden of environmental protection'.
5.6   Beckmann (1973) (*ref. 2.5*).
      Chapter 4: 'More power means more pollution: More doctors means more disease'.
5.7   Benthall, J. (ed.), *Ecology: The Shaping Enquiry*. Longmans, 1972.
      An introduction to the impact of man and technology upon nature.
5.8   Calder, Nigel (ed.), *Nature in the Round*. Weidenfeld and Nicholson, 1973.
      An introduction to environmental science.
5.9   Clarke, Richard, 'Man environment and the great growth debate', *Marxism Today*, Vol. 18, Mar.–Apr.–May 1974.
5.10 Commoner (1972) (*ref. 1.4*).
      The effects of pollution upon nature and a pessimistic view of the role of technology in society.
5.11 Cole, Lamont, 'Thermal pollution', *Bioscience*, **19**, 1969, pp. 989–992.
      The imminent danger of thermal pollution.
5.12 Daly, H. E., 'Towards a stationary state economy', in Harte and Solow (eds.), *Patient Earth*. Holt, Rinehart and Winston, 1972.

5.13 De Twyler (1971) (*ref. 3.12*).
      Describes in detail the manifold effects of pollution on
      nature.
5.14 Douglas, Mary, 'Environments at risk', a lecture given at the
      Institute of Contemporary Arts, *Times Literary Supplement.*
      30th October 1970, pp. 1275.
      A philosopher looks at the debate on pollution.
5.15 Douglas, Mary, *Purity and Danger.* Penguin, 1966.
5.16 Eckholm, Eric, *Losing Ground: Environmental Stress and World
      Food Prospects.* W. W. Norton & Co, 1976.
5.17 Ehrlich (1970) (*ref. 2.13*).
      Chapter 6: 'Environmental threats to man'.
      Chapter 7: 'Ecosystems in jeopardy'.
5.18 Environmental Studies Board (1973) (*ref. 4.11*).
      Legislation that already exists for coping with pollution.
5.19 The Ecologist (1972) (*ref. 1.5*).
      pp. 15–30, 69–116.
5.20 Falk (1971) (*ref. 4.12*).
      Chapter 2: 'The ecological imperative'.
      Chapter 3: 'Underlying causes of planetary danger'.
5.21 Farvar and Milton (eds.) (1973) (*ref. 3.20*).
5.22 Gribbin, J. (ed.), *Climatic Change.* CUP, 1978.
5.23 Heilbroner (1974) (*ref. 1.10*).
      Chapter 2: 'The external challenges'.
5.24 Kneese, Allen V., *Economics and the Environment.* NY: Penguin
      Books, 1977.
5.25 Labeyrie, Vincent, 'Crisis of environment or crisis of capitalist
      economy?', *Marxism Today*, Vol. 17, Apr. 1974.
5.26 Lecomber, R., *Economic Growth versus the Environment.*
      Macmillan Studies in Economics, 1975.
5.27 Lee, R. G., *The World Savers or Realm Savers.* University of
      California, 1970.
      Describes a middle class analysis of the present situation.
5.28 Maddox (1972) (*ref. 3.29*).
      Chapter 4: 'The pollution panic'.
      An optimistic technocratic approach to pollution.
5.29 McKnight, Allan D., Marstrand, Pauline and Sinclair, Craig T. (eds.),
      *Environmental Pollution Control: Technical, Economic and
      Legal Aspects.* George Allen and Unwin, 1974.
5.30 Mellanby, Kenneth, *The Biology of Pollution.* Edward Arnold,
      1972.
      Stresses the effects of pollution upon living organisms.
5.31 Moriarty, F., *Animals and Pollution.*
      Experiments at the Institute of Terrestrial Ecology to test the
      theories of pollutant concentration of food chains: both
      aquatic and terrestrial.

5.32 Rothman, Harry, *Murderous Providence*. Rupert Hart Davis, 1972. A study of pollution in industrial society and a Marxist defence of technological progress.

5.33 Platt, J., 'What we must do', *Science*, **166,** Nov. 1969, pp. 1115–1121.

5.34 Quigley, C., 'Our ecological crisis', *Current History*, **59**, 1970, pp. 1–12.
Other taxonomies of world crisis.

5.35 Robinson, Pauline, *The Environmental Crisis*. Communist Party, 1973.
A communist view of the crisis.

5.36 Saunders, P. J. W., *The Estimation of Pollution Damage*. Manchester Univ. Press, 1976.
An assessment of various economic methods of dealing with pollution control.

5.37 Schwartz, Mortimer D. (ed.), *Environmental Law: a guide to Information Sources*, Vol. 6 in the Man and the Environment Information Guide Series. Detroit Michigan, Gale Research Co, 1977.

5.38 Scorer, R. S., *Pollution in the Air*. Routledge and Kegan Paul, 1974.
Debunk of the polluter pays principle.

5.39 Study of Critical Environmental Problems, *Man's Impact on the Global Environment, Assessment and Recommendations for Action*. M.I.T., 1970.
The study was set up as an official USA input to the 1972 UN Conference on the Human Environment.

5.40 Sabato, J. A. and Rotana, N., 'Science and technology in the future development of Latin America', Paper to the *'World Order Models Conference'*. Italy, 1968.
Debate with growth exponents from the developing countries.

5.41 Stretton, H., *Capitalism, Socialism and the Environment*. Cambridge CUP, 1975.

5.42 *The Swedish Journal of Economics*, Vol. 73, No. 1, Mar. 1973, 'Environmental economics'.

5.43 *The First Report of the Royal Commission on Environmental Pollution*. HMSO, 1971.

5.44 US Council on Environmental Quality, *The Economic impact of pollution control: a summary of recent studies*. mimeo, 1972. (see also their annual reports 1970, 1971).

5.45 Victor, P., *Pollution Economy and Environment*. Allen and Unwin, 1972.

5.46 Worboys, M., Marstrand, P. and Lowe, P., *Science and the Environment*. (SISCON, 1974).

5.47 'Is clean power possible?', (4 articles on the subject), *New Scientist*, **63**, 26 Sept. 1974, pp. 786–803.

5.48 'Environment programme 1977—81', *Bulletin of European Communities*, 1976, supp. 6/76, whole issue.
5.49 Cohen, B. L., 'The disposal of radioactive wastes from fusion reactors', *Scientific American*, **236**, (6), June 1977, pp. 6—31.
5.50 England, R., 'Environmental gains going up in smoke', in *U. S. Capitalism in Crisis*, NY: Union of Radical Political Economists, 1978, pp. 152—154.
5.51 Esposito, John C. and Silverman, Larry J., *Vanishing Air: The Ralph Nader study group report on air pollution*. Grossman, 1970.
5.52 Lutz, R., 'The laws of environment management: a comparative study', *The Amer. J. of Comparative Law*, **24**, (3), Summer 1976, pp. 447—520.

JOURNALS

AMBIO (Oslo, Sweden — in English).
Environment.
Environmental Pollution.
Marine Pollution Bulletin.
Science of the Total Environment.

Points for discussion or essays

1—6. In the text there are a series of questions at the end of the discussion of thermal pollution, DDT and air pollution.
7. Discuss the effect of the social system upon the pollution produced. (*refs. 5.14, 5.15, 5.19, 5.22, 5.27, 5.35*).
8. Discuss the relationship between industrial society and pollution. Is global pollution a *necessary* by-product of such a society? Is it not amenable to human control? (*refs. 5.28, 5.32, 5.41*).
9. Discuss the relationship between technology and society.
10. Are people pollution?
11. Are the major sources of industrial pollution beyond the reach of social control?
12. Discuss the implications of the 'Make the Polluters Pay' principle. (*ref. 5.24, 5.36, 5.38*).
13. Industry is one of the physical sources of pollution. In order to limit pollution it has often been suggested that severe cutbacks should be made in industrial production. What are the implications of such a policy proposal. (*refs. 1.3 (pp. 66—77), 3.17, 5.9, 5.16, 5.26, 5.35, 5.51*).

QUESTIONS RELATED TO *LIMITS TO GROWTH*

1. The Pollution sub-system in the *Limits to Growth* model considers only persistent pollution which results from industrial and agricultural activity. Discuss the advantages and limitations of such a definition. (*ref. 5.1*).
2. How sound is the data base used in the pollution sub-system? (*ref. 5.1*).
3. By what criteria have the authors of *The Limits to Growth* decided that the maximum upper limit of pollution absorption will occur when the pollution level reaches 25 times that of 1970?
4. By what criteria have they decided that 100 times the present average pollution level is fatal?
5. '. . . It would be equally plausible to change the relationship in World 3 (the *Limits to Growth* model) between pollution and industrial output . . . from one which is linear to one with a diminishing marginal increase of pollution with increasing industrial output *per capita* or to one with a constant or diminishing level of pollution above a certain level of income *per capita*'. Discuss this statement. How would such a relationship affect the model output? (*ref. 5.1*).
6. Discuss the advantages and limitations of aggregating pollutants in the pollution sub-system. How important to the model is this method of dealing with pollution? Does this method affect the policies advocated to cope with pollution? (*ref. 5.1*).
7. How critical is the pollution sub-system in the *Limits to Growth* model? (*ref. 5.1*).
8. 'By aggregating all pollutants, and assuming that they behave in some composite way, attention is drawn away from what are urgent and still soluble problems, and diverted into speculation upon an imaginary race against time between 'Life' and 'Global asphyxiation'. Do you agree? (*ref. 5.1*).
9. Examine the role played by industrial production in the *Limits to Growth* model (*ref. 1.3*, pp. 66–79).

Chapter Six
The Method Used to Reach the
Conclusions of 'The Limits to Growth'

So far, we have examined in some detail several aspects of the problems tackled in *The Limits to Growth*. We have dealt with one of the two agents of disorder (population) and the three constraints to growth: food, resources and pollution.

In this chapter we will concentrate upon the methods which the authors of *The Limits to Growth* adopted to achieve their conclusions. Following this examination we will make a few comments on the general nature of large-scale models, of which *The Limits to Growth* is one example. Before continuing however, the reader is encouraged to re-read the section in the first chapter ('Limits to Growth') which was entitled 'Events leading to the publication of *The Limits to Growth*'. Such an introduction will refresh the memory as to the objectives of the authors and the reasons for their particular choice of methodology.

1. Introduction

In the introduction to *The Limits to Growth* the authors point out that

> . . . every person approaches his problems . . . with the help of models. A model is simply an ordered set of assumptions about a complex system . . . We too have used a model. Ours is a formal, written model of the world. It constitutes a preliminary attempt to improve our mental models of long term, global problems by combining the large amount of information that is already in human minds and in written records with the new information-processing tools that mankind's increasing knowledge has produced — the scientific method, systems analysis and the modern computer.

They acknowledge that the model is 'imperfect, oversimplified, and unfinished', but even so, it is 'the most useful model now available for dealing with problems far out on the space-time graph'. And as such superior to the present means by which policy makers reach decisions.

> As a formal mathematical model it also has two important advantages over mental models . . . First every assumption we make is written in a precise form so that it is open to inspection and criticism by all. Second, after the assumptions have been

scrutinized, discussed and revised to agree with our best current knowledge, their implications for the future behaviour of the world system can be traced without error by a computer no matter how complicated they become.

We feel that the advantages listed above make this model unique among all mathematical and mental world models available to us today . . . In spite of the preliminary state of our work we believe it is important to publish the model and our findings now . . . the basic behaviour modes we have already observed in this model appear to be so fundamental and general that we do not expect our broad conclusions to be substantially altered by further revisions.

Later they state how the model is important in understanding the *causes* of the limits to growth.

We see above the following assertions:
(a) the usefulness of formal models in mapping the future;
(b) the superiority of formal over mental models;
(c) the implied advantages bequeathed by the use of 'the scientific method, systems analysis and the modern computer' in constructing the model;
(d) the assumptions comprising the model are clearly displayed and open to criticism and inspection by all;
(e) the ease with which the implications of these assumptions can be traced with a computer;
(f) the model is already fit to use in policy decisions as they do not expect the broad conclusion to be altered.

During the following discussion, which is based on the views of members of the Science Policy Research Unit (SPRU), University of Sussex (*see refs. 1.3 and 6.10*), of the methods used to construct the *Limits to Growth* model, each of the above assertions will be examined.

2. Structure, methods of calculation and data base of *The Limits to Growth* model

In his critique of 'the structure of world models', in *Thinking About the Future*, Cole says:

In one sense at least Forrester's (Forrester built the prototype) and Meadow's results are incontrovertible. Exponential growth of population and industrialisation on a finite planet cannot continue indefinitely. However, they are saying much more than just this: firstly the present growth must end within the lifetime of a large proportion of the world's present population, and secondly, and more frightening, unless drastic steps are taken global disaster will occur! Their results have been given added weight because they derive from the computer, even though on the strength of their basic premise alone it is clear that exponentially growing resource use, depleting 250 year's supply of resources at present usage rates, must end rather quickly. So although one could go a long way towards verifying Forrester's and Meadow's conclusions simply by checking the underlying assumptions upon which their mathematical models are based, it is also necessary to examine the actual models in some detail. Criticisms of the model have to be computerised to be believed.

The major criticisms made by Cole and Curnow follow.

(a) THE IMPORTANT FEATURES OF THE MODEL STRUCTURE ARE:

  (i) the description of the world as a closed system with no external influences;
 (ii) the choice of the major parameters;
(iii) the major interactions and the feed back loops;
(iv) the use of world averages for all parameters;
 (v) the amount of detail (the number of relationships);
(vi) the non-probabilistic nature of its predictions.

The attempt to model the whole world is seen as avoiding the major limitation of long term forecasts: the influence of external events which have not been included in the model. However, in this case the modellers have overlooked important internal events which influence behavior in the real world: education, research and development, social and technological change in such a way as to accommodate change. In addition they have attempted to exclude mechanisms which balance social, political and economic factors in order to avoid the catastrophe anticipated by Meadows. Meadow's main argument for not including such mechanisms is that the delays in adopting new technologies or adapting to new constraints may be very long — too late to be of any use. However, this opinion, that the mechanisms will be too late to be of any use, is an assumption which *is* included in the model by the omission of such mechanisms. It is held by Cole to be invalid.

The use of world averages for all parameters: 'without dividing the model into, for instance, different geographical areas, it is impossible not to make rigid and unrealistic assumptions about the structure of distributions within the world system. Consequently it may be impossible to make sensible forecasts with such a highly aggregate model'. As to the amount of detail in the models 'most of the real world processes described (in the model) are little understood and one reason for this is that few data are available. Little is gained from the point of view of accuracy of forecasting by attempting to construct a more

99

exact model than the available data allow'. Finally the non-probabilistic nature of the predictions makes these predictions suspect. 'Processes in the real world are subject to unforeseeable fluctuations. This makes it impossible to establish relationships between variables. The use of inexact relationships and the impossibility of accounting exactly for these fluctuations precludes the possibility of making precise predictions with complete certainty. Consequently any prediction can only be attributed limited probability'.

(b) THE METHOD OF CALCULATION

Slight miscalculation of the nature of the feedback mechanisms can lead to a disruption of the dynamic balance of the model 'because errors of this kind rapidly accumulate during the step-wise calculation'. As to systems dynamics — the technique originally conceived by Forrester for programming fairly simply dynamic problems — 'although easy to use it is rather inflexible and contains approximations which can lead to errors in some circumstances'. The first comes through the way that the calculation is performed: in steps. Each calculation takes for its starting point the results of the previous calculation. Since each calculation has to 'round-off' its answers the effect of these 'rounding errors' is cumulative and in some cases significant. Another error lies in that 'the values actually taken by the multipliers in the calculation are approximations even to the assumed relationships'.

(c) DATA

'Although few "guessed" data are used the quality of much of the rest . . . is extremely poor'. Not only that but the method of choosing the data is suspect: firstly little attention has been paid to statistical methods of doing so (except in the agricultural sub-system) but more importantly:

> Many parameters used in the (model) have to date all varied simul-
> taneously and monotonically in the real world. This makes it
> difficult to separate, for example, the effects of changes in food,
> wealth, crowding and pollution on birth and death rates and to
> establish the best figures to use in the world models.

There is also the question of extrapolation: 'Serious errors of extrapolation are more likely to occur when relationships are assumed to
be multiplicative rather than additive . . . Furthermore, the fact that
a model appears to fit historical data within a certain range is not a
guarantee of the model's validity within that range, let alone an

indication that it can be used to extrapolate outside it. Many different combinations of mechanisms can give rise to the same pattern for a few major variables'.

Cole concludes his critique by saying that the 'features of the model's structure which appear to be unrealistic in a way unlikely to affect the results are the absence of technical, economic and social feedback processes and the use of world averages for all variables. Added to this is the possibility of a bias in many of the relationships arising in part from the lack of good empirical information and in part from errors of extrapolation'. The above mentioned paucity of data and the futility of constructing a more exact model than the data allow, add further cause for concern.

(d) TESTING THE MODEL

Having criticized the way in which the model was constructed, Cole and Curnow proceeded to test the validity of the claims made by the authors with regard to the model.

Firstly they find that the model does not live up to the claim that it generates trends which match historical data. This throws a certain amount of doubt on the validity of the results and any conclusions drawn from them about the future. Secondly, the authors of *The Limits to Growth* had claimed that the results of the world model were insensitive to changes in most of the assumed values of the parameters. In fact tests on the model show that it is 'very sensitive to input parameters which have a wide margin of error'. A sustained high rate of growth is just as likely as a catastrophic collapse. Thirdly, because the results are 'so sensitive to the inclusion of small rates of technological change and resource discovery (indeed the threat of *physical* limitations is removed), it seems that some very important factors have been omitted from the model'.

These and other analyses lead to a questioning of the claim that mathematical models (formal models) are necessarily superior to mental models.

(e) MENTAL AND MATHEMATICAL FORMAL MODELS

Mental modelling is the process of simplification in order to achieve conceptual clarification and understanding. In the process, details are ignored but generality may be obtained. Mathematical modelling can be used to supplement mental modelling. The consequences of assumptions derived from a mental model can be more exactly determined using the corresponding mathematical model when one can be created, although invariably in translating a mental model into a mathematical one more details and nuances are lost. A mathematical model of a process is nothing more than a set of equations which one would like to generate trends similar to those observed for the real world.

However, the MIT team argue that in understanding the behavior of complex systems, computer models have great advantages over mental models. They have also agreed with Forrester that the behavior of complex systems is in fact counter intuitive i.e. beyond the reach of mental models, and only open to understanding by dynamic formal modelling. Freeman comments that this view is unexceptionable if we are considering the number of variables, complex interactions and speed of calculation. But it can be easily exaggerated into what is best described as computer fetishism. The computer fetishist endows the computer model with a validity and an independent power which altogether transcends the mental models which are its essential basis. Because of the prevalance of this computer fetishism it cannot be repeated too often that the validity of any computer calculation depends entirely on the quality of data and assumptions (mental models) which are fed into it. Computer models cannot replace theory.

Cole and Curnow also challenge the superiority of mathematical over mental models after their analysis of the *Limits to Growth* model. Since the data are poor, it is all too easy 'for a systematic bias reflecting a particularly pessimistic (or for that matter optimistic) view to influence the actual estimates used'. This is proven by the way in which the results of the model were changed 'radically by altering a few of the principal assumptions' (Cole and Curnow in *ref. 6.2*, pp. 125–131). . . . 'according to World 3 a high rate of growth is just as likely as a catastrophic collapse' (Cole and Curnow, p. 130).

The claim that computer models are superior to mental models is not borne out by the model itself. 'Decision makers concerned with say, pollution control, agriculture or natural resources might have very simplified and imperfect mental models but, given their firsthand knowledge of the subject matter, they might also have avoided the rather elementary mistakes made in the assumptions (of the model)'.

Further 'much of the complexity is false': from the results of the world model 'even with high complex dynamic systems the important behavior at any time or under any circumstances is usually dominated by relatively few parameters'.

And it is not possible to accept Meadow's assertion that the need to formalize each interaction of the system modelled ensures that every assumption can be critically examined and discussed. Furthermore these models are not open to inspection by all since this inspection requires access to large scale computer facilities.

Dr. R. Golub, a physicist at Sussex, has argued that the MIT approach is inherently dangerous since it encourages self-delusion in five ways:
(i) by giving the spurious appearance of precise knowledge of quantities and relationships which are unknown and in many cases unknowable;

(ii) by encouraging the neglect of factors which are difficult to quantify such as policy changes or value changes;

(iii) by stimulating gross oversimplification, because of the problem of aggregation and the comparative simplicity of our computers and mathematical techniques;

(iv) by encouraging the tendency to treat some features of the model as rigid and immutable;

(v) by making it extremely difficult for the non-numerate or those who do not have access to computers to rebut what are essentially tendentious and rather naive political assumptions.

(f) OBJECTIVITY OF THE MODEL

In relation to data, Freeman has written that the MIT team are not responsible for the lack of data but that they may be criticized for trying to erect such an elaborate theoretical structure and such sweeping conclusions on so precarious a data base. He continues that by Meadow's own admission only about 0.1% of the data on the variables required to construct a satisfactory model is now available. Little is known about the forces which determined past relationships between some of the variables: still less about their future relationships. This has meant that the modellers were required to make assumptions about relationships and to make estimates about data. There are many possible assumptions about such a complex system as the future of the human race. Consequently the MIT team has had to choose between alternative assumptions. Moreover since the world is so complex they had to omit what they consider to be irrelevant. These decisions are matters of judgement, not of fact or mathematics. For example, the MIT team tried to concentrate on physical limits to growth and omit changes in values, yet these changes may be the most important dynamic element in the whole system.

The assumptions and judgements made by the computer modellers depend no less than those of other scientists on their mental models — on their information, their bias, their experience and their values. What is on a computer printout depends on the assumptions which are made about the real world relationships and these assumptions in turn are heavily influenced by the contemporary social theories and values to which the computer modellers are exposed. The nature of their assumptions is not a purely technical problem. Political bias and values are implicitly or explicitly present in any study of the social system. The apparent detached neutrality of a computer model is as illusory as it is persuasive. Any model of any social system *necessarily* involves assumptions about the workings of that system and these assumptions are necessarily colored by the attitudes and values of the individual or groups concerned. Freeman's conclusion was that the critique of a computer model is not just a question of looking at the structure, or conducting mathematical tests. 'Far more important is the examination of the underlying assumptions'. What does emerge from the analysis of the model itself is that 'the work of modellers (and their critics) should not be viewed as a totally objective or apolitical statement of real world situations. Neither should modellers pretend that it is'.

Finally, the objectivity of *The Limits to Growth* must be considered in the light of the following. After the formation of the Club of Rome in 1968, club members had, for two years, 'plodded quietly from Moscow to Rio, from Stockholm to Washington, seeking out political leaders and appraising them of the dangers ahead'. Peccei wrote 'Our message was received with sympathy and understanding, but no action followed'. And so, in his own words:

> Clearly the inertia keeping society on the present course is a formidable force. Other more powerful and comprehensive tools of communication and conviction than those now used were necessary if world public opinion and policy makers were to be moved . . . tools which would reflect the inherent complexity of the message the Club of Rome wants to put through and yet have a strong, lasting impact on people's minds. Professor Forrester of MIT . . . thought that he could forge one such tool by upgrading his systems dynamics techniques . . . and make them applicable to nothing less than the entire world system.

(g) THE USE OF MODELS IN POLICY MAKING

Finally the members of SPRU are not wholly convinced that world models based on system dynamics can develop into satisfactory tools of forecasting and policy making. They regard it as still a question for experiment and discussion, whereas the MIT team is prepared to base a prescription for the world on the results of their model.

Nevertheless, with reservations such as these mentioned above, they believe that the attempt to develop satisfactory mathematical models is worthwhile and can be a valuable aid to systematic thought. It may prove difficult for a long time to overcome the justifiable objections which can be raised and they would certainly approach all social systems models with great scepticism. Any attempt to represent future tendencies in the world, whether in words or in numbers is attended by great difficulties. They nevertheless believe such attempts to be of great importance, whether in the arts or in the sciences. Even if their judgement on the particular MIT model is largely negative, they see some point in its existence in the sense of its being a stimulus to a fundamental debate.

3. General discussion of large scale models

Since the publication of *The Limits to Growth* there has been a 'revived interest in the possibilities of using large scale computer models for the forecasting of long term futures'. Cole, in association with Clark, Curnow, Freeman, Jahoda and Hopkins, has been stimulated by this revived interest to write an article entitled 'Limitations of large scale models in forecasting'. In this article he states that the perceived advantages of large scale models are:

   (a) they offer a means of testing and exploring policy options without damaging the real world where the possibilities for experimentation are highly constrained — possibilities of designing and testing alternative social futures.
   (b) the systems which the large scale models attempt to describe are highly integrated and cannot easily or satisfactorily be reduced into descriptions of their component parts separately.

Over the past decade large scale models have been already built and used in two areas — national economic planning and urban planning. Cole decided in starting his discussion of large scale world models that it would be sensible to examine the success of these models in the areas where they had already been tried and tested. In the case of economic models he found (i) despite the fact that the models are based on at least a ten year period of the best social data their predictive power is limited to only a few quarters (of the year); (ii) they are difficult to calibrate and test so tend to be judged by the extent to which reality matches prediction; (iii) they are limited to forecasting economic performance in quantitative terms and (iv) extreme difficulties were involved in modelling across political divides; so far economic models have been used only within nations.

For urban models, however, he found that large scale models were sometimes viewed as a 'disaster': 'After a decade or more of considerable expenditure and effort, little has been gained either from the point of view of the city or regional planner, or according to Lee, even in terms of understanding of the working of the urban social environment'. Another critic has listed 'seven sins' of urban models: Hypercomprehensiveness, Grossness, Hungriness (for data), Wrongheadedness, Complicatedness, Mechanicalness, Expensiveness. Finally the main constraints upon urban models have been found to be institutional. The real progress in urban models probably awaits the emergence of better social theories.

Having examined the results of large scale modelling in urban and national economic planning, Cole turned his attention to the global and ecological modelling that has taken place over the last few years. Besides *The Limits to Growth* there are now at least six models being constructed at institutes in Europe, America (South and North) and Japan. In general he found the following:

(a) Technically they are 'extremely difficult to manage in construction, calibration, evaluation and application';

(b) The data and social theory are hardly sufficiently developed to 'bear the weight of such a large model';

(c) Institutional difficulties — which modellers must learn to take into account if their work is to be more than just an interesting exercise — present even more formidable obstacles to the modellers than the technical difficulties.

In addition to the above he has further comments related to large scale models:

(a) On models themselves:

  (i) Too much attempted in a single model. Even the claim that formally structuring a problem leads to clarification is often not true as practiced simply because of extraneous detail;

  (ii) The apparent rationality and objectivity of models is appealing but it can hide quite dubious assumptions concerning, for example, measurement of parameters, or invalid scales, or it can imply a consensus of views which does not exist;

  (iii) Models are often at the same time simplistic (i.e. results could be predicted without a computer) and unmanageable (i.e. too many variables);

  (iv) Large scale models are slow to develop and require a large empirical data base. But when details are changed they need extensive recalibration and their usefulness can be easily affected by the change in definition of the problem (even fashion);

  (v) Diminishing returns to complexity.

(b) On the difficulty of incorporating social and institutional factors:

  (i) Social issues are so complex that large scale models have been unable to help and have added to the confusion;

  (ii) A successful computer model requires a good basis of theory and data which is normally only achieved over a considerable period of time. Simply because this time has elapsed in data collection, interest groups with entrenched positions have come into being and often tend to frustrate compromise;

  (iii) There is a long way to go before even complex 'physical' processes, where all relationships are in principle known, can be adequately described — good models of global weather systems and the more complex industrial processes are beyond our current abilities. In social systems there is an added dimension of complexity in that the relationships between components are constantly changing and that in any event social theories are more controversial than their physical counterparts;

(c) On the use of models:
    (i) Will they be used? For a policy maker to tie his political future to a model means firstly confidence in the model's assumptions and secondly confidence in the way the model manipulates those assumptions;
    (ii) Implications of 'the existence of a "managerial" style of planning is almost a precursor to a successful public policy model', are that this 'could lead to a technocratic and insensitive style of control';
    (iii) Computer models produce an air of inevitability — if used in policy, if the forecast is negative, there are dangers of a self-fulfilling prophecy.

The overall impression of these comments is that large scale world models have so far had extreme limitations. Cole does however see a future for them in ecology, meteorology and oceanography. He lightens the blow by adding:

> many widely used economic models, for example, input-output analysis and Keynesian models, were highly controversial at one time so that scepticism of global models may be misplaced when viewed in historical context.

But finally, Cole and his five colleagues advocate the use of smaller, focused, less elaborate models.

In conclusion

Elsewhere, in relation to their critique of the *Limits to Growth* model itself the authors of *Thinking About the Future* have written:

> Since the criticism is extensive, and sometimes severe, it is essential to make several points quite clear at the outset.
> First, although the authors of the essays disagree strongly with much of the MIT analysis they are in complete agreement with the MIT authors and their sponsors, the Club of Rome, about the urgency of many of the social problems with which they are concerned, such as population growth rates, the development of satisfactory national and international mechanisms for the monitoring and prevention of pollution hazards and conservation of amenity.
> Secondly, as the paper by Cole makes clear, their critique should not be taken as an attack on the use of mathematical model-building in the social sciences. On the contrary, the social sciences can benefit from the use of computer model-building techniques and specifically from systems dynamics. However,

such models also have serious limitations and dangers of mis-use.

Thirdly they do not under-estimate the positive importance of the MIT work as a courageous and pioneering attempt. As a result of reading *The Limits to Growth* many people are now thinking anew about long-term problems and discussing them much more seriously. This is a very important achievement.

Since time immemorial men have attempted to predict the future. In one sense *The Limits to Growth* is merely another attempt. But the popularity of *The Limits to Growth* (it has sold nearly 2,000,000 copies) and the developments which led to its publication show that it expresses deeply felt sentiments of the early seventies and as such it is as much a mirror of its own time as a forecast of the future.

Reading

ESSENTIAL

6.1   Cole, H. S. D., 'The structure of world models', in Cole *et al.* (1973) (*ref. 1.3*), pp. 14–32.
6.2   Cole, H. S. D. and Curnow, R. C., 'An evaluation of world models', in Cole *et al.* (1973) (*ref. 1.3*), pp. 108–134.
6.3   Freeman, Christopher, 'Malthus with a computer', in Cole *et al.* (1973) (*ref. 1.3*), pp. 5–13.
6.4   Meadows *et al.* (1972) (*ref. 1.1*), 'Introduction', pp. 20–23, 88–91.
6.5   Golub, R. and Townsend, J., 'Malthus multinationals and the Club of Rome', *Social Studies of Science*, 7, 1977, pp. 201–222.

ADDITIONAL (includes material on the whole *Limits* debate)

6.6   Arab-Ogly, E., *In the Forecaster's Maze*. Moscow Progress Publishers, 1975.
6.7   Barnes, E., *Scientific Knowledge and Social Theory*. London: Routledge and Kegan Paul, 1974.
6.8   Beckmann (1973) (*ref. 2.5*). Chapter 5: 'The computerized soothsayers', pp. 152–179.
6.9   Clarke, John and Cole, Sam, *Global Simulation Models – A Comparative Study*. John Wiley, 1975.
6.10 Cole, H. S. D., in association with Clark, J., Curnow, R., Freeman, C., Jahoda, M. and Hopkins, M., 'Limitations of large scale models in forecasting'. Mimeo SPRU, 1974.

6.11 Connelly, P. and Perlman, R., *The Politics of Scarcity: Resources Conflicts in International Relations.* The Royal Institute of International Affairs by OUP, 1975.

6.12 Easlea, B. (1973) (*ref. 4.8*).

6.13 Easterlin, R. A., 'Does economic growth improve the human lot? Some empirical evidence', in P. A. David and M. W. Reader (eds.), *Nations and Households in Economic Growth.* London: Academic Press, 1974.

6.14 Encel, S., Marstrand, P. K. and Page, W., *The Art of Anticipation.* London: Martin Robertson, 1975.

6.15 Freeman and Jahoda (eds.) (1978) (*ref. 1.8*).

6.16 Forrester (1971) (*ref. 1.7*).

6.17 Herrera *et al.* (1976) (*ref. 1.11*).

6.18 Hirsch, Fred, *The Social Limits to Growth.* Camb. Mass: Harvard UP

6.19 Kahn *et al.* (1977) (*ref. 1.12*).

6.20 Kayser, Carl, 'The computer that printed out W*O*L*F', *Foreign Affairs,* **50,** (4), July 1972, pp. 660–668.

6.21 Leontief *et al.* (1976) (*ref. 1.13*).

6.22 Mesarovic and Pestel (1974) (*ref. 1.16*).

6.23 Ophuls, W., *Ecology and the Politics of Scarcity.* Prologue to a political theory of the steady state. San Francisco: W. H. Freeman and Co., 1977.

6.24 O'Riordan, *Environmentalism.* London: Pion Ltd., Research in Planning and Design series, 1976.

6.25 Peccei, Aurelio, *The Human Quality.* Pergamon, 1977. Depicts 'a future world community governed by intelligent, concerned rational people – the new humanists'.

6 26 Ravetz, J., *Scientific Knowledge and its Social Problems.* Oxford: Clarendon Press, 1971.

6.27 Rose, H. and Rose, S., *Science and Society.* Penguin, 1969.

6 28 Rose, H. and Rose, S. (eds.), *The Political Economy of Science: ideology in the natural sciences.* Macmillan, 1976.

6.29 Saunders, Robert S., 'Criticism and the growth of knowledge: An examination of the controversy over *The Limits to Growth',* *Stanford Journal of International Studies,* **IX,** Spring 1974, pp. 45–70.

6.30 Sauvy, A., *Zero Growth?,* Oxford: Blackwell, 1975.

6.31 Scolnik, Hugo D., 'On a methodological criticism of the Meadows World 3 Model'. Fundacion Bariloche, 1974.

6.32 Simmons, H. G., 'Systems dynamics and technocracy', in Cole *et al.* (1973) (*ref. 1.3*), pp. 192–208.

6.33 Stretton, H., *Capitalism, Socialism and the Environment.* Cambridge CUP, 1975.

6.34 Tinbergen (coordinator) and Dolman (ed.) (1976) (*ref. 1.18*).

6.35 'Growth and the future', *Policy Sciences,* **5,** June 1974, pp. 129–236 (whole issue on growth).

6.36 *Social Science Quarterly*, **57**, (2), Sept. 1976.
Special issue on 'Scarcity and Society'.

6.37 'Limits to growth "75" from physical to socio-economic limits',
Futures, **8**, (6), Dec. 1976, pp. 509—16.

6.38 Ashby, E., 'On Club of Rome's 'dynamics of growth in a finite
world" ', *Nature*, 22 Jan. 1975, pp. 170.

6.39 Ashby, E., 'Futurologist's examined', *Nature*, 9 Nov. 1978,
pp. 144—146.
A review of Freeman & Jahoda (ed.) (1978) *World Futures*.

6.40 Atkinson, P. and Kusch, J., 'Limits to growth or limits to
capitalism?', *Science for the People*, No. 33, (1976), pp. 12—14.

6.41 Cole, S., *Global Models and the International Economic Order*,
Pergamon, 1977.

6.42 Freeman, C., 'The luxury of despair: a reply to Robert Heilbroner's
"Human Prospect" ', *Futures*, **6**, (6), 1974, pp. 450—62.

6.43 Fyodorov, Y., 'Growth will go on', *Development Forum*, **VI**, (3),
Apr. 1978, pp. 1—2.

6.44 James, J., 'Growth, technology and the environment in less
developed countries: a survey', *World Development*, **6**, (7/8),
July/Aug. 1978, pp. 137—165.

6.45 Heilbroner, R., 'Boom and crash', *The New Yorker*, 28 Aug.
1978, pp. 52—73 (see especially pp. 70—3 for use of *Limits*
conclusions).

6.46 Lara, F. and Sachs, W. M., 'Modelling of the environment through
a system of models', *Applied Mathematical Modelling*, **2**, (3),
Sept. 1978, pp. 216—9.

6.47 Meadows, D. H. and D. L., 'Typographical errors and technological
solutions', *Nature*, 11 Jan. 1974, pp. 97—8.

6.48 Miles, I., 'Ideologies of Futurists', in Fowles, J. (ed.), *Handbook
of Futures Research*, Greenwood Press, 1978, pp. 67—97.
The *Handbook* also contains articles by Bell, Brown, Clarke,
Commoner, Ferkiss and Forrester.

6.49 Miles, I. and Irvine, J., 'Social forecasting: predicting the future
or making history', in Irvine, J., Miles, I. and Evans, J.,
Demystifying Social Statistics, Pluto Press, 1979.

6.50 O'Riordan, T., 'Environmental ideologies', *Environment and
Planning*, **9**, (1), Jan. 1977, pp. 3—14.

6.51 Poquet, G., 'The limits to global modelling', *International Social
Science Journal*, **XXX**, (2), 1978, pp. 284—300.

6.52 Richardson, J., 'Global modelling — 1: The Models', *Futures*, **10**,
(5), Oct. 1978, pp. 386—404.

JOURNALS

As for Chapter One plus:
Applied Mathematical Modelling.
Long-range Planning.

Points for discussion or essays

1. 'Criticisms of the model have to be computerized to be believed'. Why?
2. Discuss the relative merits of mental and mathematical modelling.
3. Discuss the neutrality of computer models.
4. 'The MIT team cannot be blamed for the lack of data, although they may be critized for trying to erect such an elaborate theoretical structure and such sweeping conclusions on so precarious a data base'. Nothing ventured nothing gained. Is this a fair criticism?
5. 'Meadows himself has emphasized that only about 0.1% of the data on the variables required to construct a satisfactory world model is now available'. Discuss.
6. 'Since ours is a formal, or mathematical, model it also has two important advantages over mental models. First, every assumption we make is written in a precise form so that it is open to inspection by all. Second, after the assumptions have been scrutinized, discussed, and revised to agree with our best current knowledge, their implications for the future behavior of the world system can be traced without error by computer, no matter how complicated they become'. Do you agree? Why?
7. Hugo Scolnik has written:

    The purpose of this article is to show that . . . continual growth can be obtained not by the introduction of . . . further assumptions, which necessarily imply some value judgments about the continuation of technical progress, but that it can be obtained by a combination of extremely small perturbations within the given structure and data of the model itself. Indeed, the magnitude of the perturbations is certainly insignificant when judged against the uncertainty of estimation admitted in *The Limits to Growth*.

    It will now be shown that continued population growth without catastrophic decline can be achieved up to at least the year 2300 AD by extremely minor, i.e. less than 5%, changes to the actual values of the parameters used in the World 3 Model. It is not argued that this will be the pattern of the real world, but rather than the previous conclusions drawn by the originators and sponsors of World 3 are unnecessarily pessimistic and are in no sense a unique conclusion from that work, since comparatively optimistic conclusions could equally well have been made.

Comment on these statements vis-a-vis *The Limits to Growth*.

8. Have the conclusions of *The Limits to Growth* been used as a starting point for (a) academics (b) policy-makers? (*refs. 1.8, 1.10, 2,4, 6.45*). Name and discuss.

9. The authors of *The Limits to Growth* state that scientific method is one of the new information processing tools used to construct the model. An introduction to discussion of science and scientific method may be gained by reference to *6.7, 6.12, 6.26, 6.27, 6.28.*

10. Materials for a seminar on the political and ideological aspects of *The Limits to Growth* debate are contained in bibliographies of earlier chapters. A starting point could be the article by B. Golub and J. Townsend. (*ref. 6.5*). Further material would be found in *refs. 6.3, 6.6, 6.8, 6.11, 6.14, 6.18, 6.23, 6.24, 6.25, 6.29, 6.30, 6.33, 6.41.*

11. The end of *Mankind at the Turning Point* is followed by a commentary written by Peccei and King. The final paragraph reads:

> It is for these reasons that we recommend this report to the political class and to the public. At the same time, we express the hope that resources be made available to develop further these techniques so that those of us who have the tremendous responsibility of making major decisions at this turn of history be aided to make them in the true interest of the peoples of the world, today and tomorrow.

To which reasons and techniques do they refer? What relation to 'we' and 'us' bear to you or I? (*refs. 6.22, 6.25* and refs for 10 above).

12. Refer back to Chapter One, Essay topic 14. If necessary rewrite your summary of *The Limits to Growth*.

13. '*The Limits to Growth* is not just a book, it is an event. It seems safe to say, that it will serve for the early 1970s the role which Michael Herrington's *The Other America* served for the early 1960s — it will open eyes, stimulate studies, start fights and affect public policies'.

Do you agree? Had you heard of *The Limits to Growth* before beginning this course? Does your answer tell more about yourself or about *The Limits to Growth*.